Cover photo compliments of Karl and Beth Kurz

Author's photo on back cover © Alisa Murray Photography 2008

ALL GOD MOMENTS ® by the Holy Spirit (thanks Wayne!)

Published by NICE FISH PUBLISHING, LLC 2011

Printed in the USA by BookMasters, Ashland, Ohio

LIFE IS SIMPLE...

IT'S JUST NOT EASY

In memory of
John Gordon and
Joan Clavell Muir

**"Dad, when we have kids, we're going to send them
to you and mom so you can discipline them."**

Wow, my daughters actually want my wife and me to influence their children? Really? What an honor to have your children desire to have you influence their children. But wait; what if something happens to me and/or Debbie tomorrow, and we don't have the opportunity to influence our grandchildren? And what about our great-grandchildren? David, why don't you write down a few thoughts so that they have something to remember?

OK, good idea. So let's write down a few thoughts on parenting? Yes, that is good, but wait! Before becoming a good parent, don't you have to become a good spouse? Well of course! After all, a good marriage is the foundation for a good family. So yes, you'd better put down something on marriage.

But wait! Before becoming a good spouse, you must become a mature adult ready to handle both the blessings and the responsibilities of marriage and parenthood. Right?

Whoa. This is starting to get a bit heavy. Now that I think about it, life is heavy! This is serious business. Committing your life to another…i.e. marriage, and raising your children to be the future leaders…yes, this is a big deal!

But wait! What about something bigger? Before you can really achieve your full potential in life and reach maturity as intended by our Creator, don't you have to get in touch with your eternal plan? Don't you have to get to know Who created you in the first place? So we'd better include a bit on our heavenly Father, Who created everything!

So what began as a harmless request for help raising our future grandchildren over the dinner table one evening has arrived where everything begins, and that is with God Himself. He is the ultimate source for instruction on how we should live our life.

So please, please, please, test everything I or anyone else has to say against God's Word, the Bible, for He is our ultimate authority, and He deserves all the credit.

I am simply a man who has a desire help others. My wife and I are putting down our personal perspective on how God's Truth works out in our life. So here we are. I took the lead on this project to write down what I believe is very SIMPLE stuff on life. SIMPLE...yes...but NOT EASY!

Acknowledgements

So before I begin, I'd like to first acknowledge my wife Debbie and our three daughters, Lauren, Heather, and Amanda for their love, support, and assistance in completing this project. In addition, there are so many special people the Lord has placed in our lives to bless us beyond measure. Specifically I want to thank our parents, John Gordon and Joan Clavell Muir along with Bill and Norma Adamcik, for providing Debbie and I with Christian-based homes from which to grow and mature. Then there are our siblings and extended family members who have shared life with us and poured into us in wonderful ways only close family can. Specifically for this book, Kelley and Wayne Kerr have been a constant source of encouragement and coaching to get us to the finish line. And then there are so many strong and gifted spiritual mentors that have personally cultivated truth in our lives: Fred Lybrand, Jim Leggett, Paul

Helbig, again Kelley and Wayne Kerr, Jeff Campbell, Kelly Needham, Mitch Pearson, and Nolan Donald. And to our extended church family at Grace, our Adult Small Group, my fellow D-Group leaders and young men and women of God at RPM, and all those in our current church family, Grace Fellowship, as well as our previous church family at Midland Bible, to my Saturday morning men's prayer group (loved those pancakes…the fellowship wasn't too bad either!), all my golfing and fishing buddies, to the Pine Cove Christian Camp Family, and especially to those spiritual mentors in my immediate family…thank you all for allowing the Lord to use you to impact my spiritual growth along with my wife and three daughters, to change lost & hardened hearts into followers of Jesus Christ, to make the Lord's name famous, and bring glory to God. I pray you continue to be Christ-centered, Christ-lead, God-glorifying members of the body of Christ.

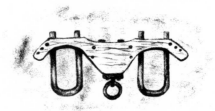

Life is Simple...It's Just Not Easy

Contents

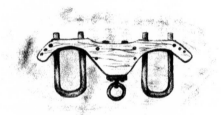

Chapter 1: PURPOSE

Here is where everything begins and ends: life can be "Simple" and "Easier" if you practice the following...

"Take my yoke upon you and learn from Me...
...For My yoke is easy and My burden light"
Matthew 11:28-30

I. Expectations...What you can expect from this book?
Encouragement to *give the most* out of this life and in the process *receive the most*, to have hope for the future and for eternity, provocation to change yourself and your circumstances for the better, to grow and to sow seeds of joy, to laugh a little along the way, to share a bit of my life story, and finally to demonstrate the manifestation of Biblical truth and the power of the Holy Spirit in practical life experiences in hopes it will help you constructively benefit yourself and the world around you.

II. Audience…Who did I write this book for?
My children, their children, their children's children, and so on. I'm interested in making things better for those around me. I have a strong belief that simply put, if you have solid relationships with the Lord and with others, always seek to do your best, live J-O-Y-fully, never lose, accept and take accountability for the decisions you make, stop complaining, live in freedom, and approach your marriage and parenting from the proper perspective, your life has a chance of being better, a lot better. Some have told me others might be interested in what I have to say. So here we are. Having said that…

I am not a fan of wasting time, yours or mine. This book was written for people who want the following package, which I'll call "Package A":
- to learn and become a responsible adult
- to lengthen the days of your life
- to be at peace in your relationships
- to have a clear path toward the future
- to have favor with God and man…This is <u>REALLY IMPORTANT</u>!

And just to be clear, this book is probably not for those who want the following package, which I'll call "Package B":
- to take the more difficult road of learning primarily from their own experiences
- to take unnecessary risks for the short-term and jeopardize the future for self and others
- to take short cuts, coast through life, and realize less than your full potential
- to live for self and avoid investing in relationships with God and man

So what about you? Which package are you more interested in: A or B? If you more interested in Package B, then perhaps this book is not for you. However, if you're interested in Package A, then I invite you to read on.

III. Disclosure...

Before going any further, you must understand something very important. In fact, it is the most important part of this entire "Simple – Not Easy" message about life:

You and I cannot fully understand or live out the things discussed in this book on our own.

You're going to read some ideas and truth in the pages ahead and think to yourself, "I can't possibly do that!" And I'll have to agree with you. You and I cannot if we're doing this alone. We need some assistance in order to see clearly, have the proper motivation, and be empowered to live life to the fullest. So where does this assistance come from?

It comes from the indwelling of God's Holy Spirit and surrendering to His control.

What I am about to discuss is really not from me. It is God's Truth lived out in His power. It's really a very simple approach to life:

Let go and Let God

If you are a believer in Jesus Christ, thanks and praise be to God for you are already equipped and have all you need. The question for believers in Christ is this:

Is God "resident" in your life or is He "president" of your life?

You see, if you have received Christ, He has taken up "residence" in your heart (see Chapter 2 for more). However, until you allow Him to lead you through the Holy Spirit will He become "president" in your life. That will make a difference, a big difference!

And if you have not yet accepted Jesus Christ's shed blood for the forgiveness of sin and placed your faith in Jesus for your eternal salvation, then my prayer for you is to consider the following questions and genuinely seek answers:

- What is the purpose of life? What is your purpose?
- Where are you going, both in this life and beyond?

If you don't want to answer those questions, then I challenge you to consider the following:

How does life begin? How did your life begin?

Think with me for a moment and ponder how can a fully functioning human being such as you or I - with multiple senses (taste, touch, hearing, smell, sight), multiple and integrated bodily systems (skeletal, muscular, circulatory, digestive, nervous...), unique physical features (skin/eye/hair color, height, build, etc.), unique personalities, emotions, and perhaps most amazing of all, cognitive and mental abilities via an amazingly sophisticated brain - come into being by simply combining a female egg with a male sperm? How does one take these two cells, which by themselves remain unchanged, however, when combined, trigger an amazing chain reaction of cell divisions that know exactly what to do and when and in what sequence in order to form all the systems, features, and cognitive capacities integrated perfectly into a fully functioning human being? And what about the heart; why does it start beating and what makes it continue? How does it know how fast to beat? And don't even get me started about DNA, the ultra complex genetic code that somehow programs the cells how to form. Look at your hand. How can your brain somehow communicate via a nervous system to open and close your hand? You do realize what's actually going on when you "move" your hand? Your brain is sending electrical impulses through your nervous system to your muscles which in turn cause the muscles to contract and relax thus opening and closing your hand. What regulates these electrical impulses? How do the impulses know which nerves to travel down to connect to the right set of muscles to allow you to use your hand? Do you "think" about it or does it just happen? And consider the magnitude and complexity of these brain-to-muscle signals as you watch an accomplished basketball, football, tennis, or soccer player move their bodies effortlessly as they perform. I'm actually typing this very minute the words you are reading; how do I take thoughts from my brain and then use my fingers in just the right key strokes to accurately "write down" my thoughts and communicate with you? Truly amazing! What about the eye? How does light refracted through the lens somehow translate into electrical impulses in your optic nerve that when sent again via the nervous system to the brain get reformatted into a clear and colorful picture that you "see"? You're "seeing" the symbols on this page that when placed in the proper sequence, represent words which then translate my thoughts to you. Did you get that? You're "seeing" and "reading" my thoughts! That's miraculous if you really think about it. And what makes your skin only grow so thick? What keeps it together? Your body is made up of 75% water. Why don't we all just pour out on the ground like a spilled glass of water? Why do we have 2 sexes? Which sex came first and how does that work if you need both sexes to form a human being? How did this all come to be? Was it an accident, a random chance, or intelligent design? I could go on an on about the complexities and marvels of the human body and it's a subject I find fascinating. My point:

You don't have to go beyond <u>the miracle of you</u> to get a glimpse of the awesome majesty of our Creator.

And guess what, you were made in His image! Did you hear that? Don't believe me, why don't we ask Him?

"Then God said, 'Let Us make man in Our image, according to Our likeness...'" Genesis 1:26a

The truth is that God made you in His image and His likeness! If you are serious about realizing your full potential as an individual, as a spouse, as a parent, as a masterpiece created by God, then please consider the questions from page 4 and genuinely seek answers. While the concepts written in the pages ahead may spark some interest,

...until you have the Spirit of the Living God you won't be able to fully understand nor have the power to live out the "Simple – Not Easy life."

My prayer is that you will earnestly seek and He promises the following:

"Ask, and it will be given to you; seek, and you will find; knock, and it will be opened to you. For everyone who asks receives, and he who seeks finds, and to him who knocks it will be opened."

Jesus Christ   Matthew 7:7-8

IV. Motivations...So what motivated me to write this book?

"My son, do not forget my teaching, But let your heart keep my commandments; for length of days and years of life And peace they will add to you. Do not let kindness and truth leave you; bind them around your neck, write them on the tablet of your heart. So you will find favor and good repute in the sight of God and man. Trust in the LORD with all your heart and do not lean on your own understanding. In all your ways acknowledge Him, and He will make your paths straight. Do not be wise in your own eyes; fear the LORD and turn away from evil."   Proverbs 3:1-7

"Hear, O Israel! The LORD is our God, the LORD is one! You shall love the LORD your God with all your heart and with all your soul and with all your might. These words, which I am commanding you today, shall be on your heart. You shall teach them diligently to your sons and shall talk of them when you sit in your house and when you walk by the way and when you lie down and when you rise up. You shall bind them as a sign on your hand and they shall be as frontals on your forehead. You shall write them on the doorposts of your house and on your gates."   Deuteronomy 6:4-9

"A wise man learns from his own mistakes. A wiser man learns from the mistakes of others." *(anonymous)*

Motivation 1:

To pass on what I know to others: that life is simple, it's just not easy!

I believe that life can be very simple. But I must add rather quickly, that does not mean that life is easy. In fact, I would say the opposite is true:

Life in general is challenging and requires effort on your part.

Oh sure from time to time things can seem easy. But for the most part, life just isn't easy. Whether you agree with me or not, life will always have its challenges for me, for you, for everybody. The question is, whether you or I will add to the already **uneasiness of life** by seeking short cuts, making life more complicated, complex, confusing, anxious, overly stressful, unbalanced, and at times just too much?

You see, the world says that life can be easy. Just do this or that and then afterwards all will be simple and easy, no more struggling required, you can coast from there. Consider what Jesus had to say about making life easy for yourself and coasting:

> And He told them a parable, saying, "The land of a rich man was very productive. And he began reasoning to himself, saying, 'What shall I do, since I have no place to store my crops?' Then he said, 'This is what I will do: I will tear down my barns and build larger ones, and there I will store all my grain and my goods. 'And I will

say to my soul, "Soul, you have many goods laid up for many years to come; take your ease, eat, drink and be merry."' But God said to him, 'You fool! This very night your soul is required of you; and now who will own what you have prepared?' So is the man who stores up treasure for himself, and is not rich toward God."

Jesus Christ   Luke 12:16-21

The world's falsehood that "life can be easy" sounds so promising, so compassionate, so hopeful, so good, so desirable, but the truth is that it just isn't reality. We aspire to make life as easy as possible. We all do it, and I'm not advocating we make life more difficult than it should be. I'd even go so far to say that **if there is a better way to do something that is more efficient, helps others, and creates benefit and value for the world around you, then by all means make the world a better place.** However, if you buy into the falsehood that life for you as an individual can be easy, then you will be tempted to think short-term and take short cuts, bringing with it unnecessary risk, relational strain, and added complexity which compounds upon itself and in the end brings even more uneasiness into our lives and unfortunately to the lives of those around us. If you don't believe me, then consider a few analogies to demonstrate the point:

(a) Sports
(b) Education
(c) Financial Success
(d) Relationships

(a) Sports: We all love sports, right? What significant, well known, fan-favorite athlete with sustained, long-term performance did not work very hard to achieve their fitness, skill level, and competitive achievements? Did they get there by sitting on the couch and wasting their time? How much effort did they exert when training or competing? Did they take short cuts or bend the rules? Was it easy for them to train, eat right, study, strategize, persevere, learn, and be pushed to their limit both physically and mentally in the heat of competition? What about the opposite? What happens to good athletes who take short-cuts, such as slack off with their training, over extend their bodies through poor diet and lack of rest, cheat or bend the rules, or worse, take drugs to enhance performance? And when unwise choices are made, are the consequences limited to just the individual who made the choice, or does it impact coaches, teammates, family, fans and close friends?

Personal Story: I was overweight as a child because I enjoyed my mom's cooking a bit excessively and chose not have a very active lifestyle. As a result, I was viewed as uncoordinated, slow and lacking confidence with athletic activities. I was the kid who was picked last for a team. For me it had nothing to do with ability, it had to do with personal choice. The summer before entering high school, I had finally had enough, and through the encouragement of my family, in particular my mom and older brothers, I improved my diet and began to run. I lost 25 lbs that summer and have been enjoying the benefits of a healthier diet, running and many other physical activities ever since. Oh, and I still enjoy home cooking…a lot!

> "Do you not know that those who run in a race all run, but only one receives the prize? Run in such a way that you may win."   1Corinthians 9:24

(b) Education: How many of us already knew how to read, write, and do arithmetic from the day we were born? Or how to operate a PC or a cell phone? We all go through the learning process. The question is, how well have you and I done? Show me a good student over *a long period of time*, and I'll show you someone who is diligent, consistent, goes to class, does their homework, studies well before tests, most likely has a good relationship with the teacher, and **helps those around them learn as well.** Sure there are some of us that are more gifted than others and academics seem to come easier for some. Easier maybe, but never easy. You see, to reach your full potential, it requires effort over the long-term for everyone, those gifted and those not-so-gifted. The way I see it, the gifted ones academically should learn more and faster because they have been given the talent to do so. Anyone gifted or not, that chooses to procrastinate, skip classes or assignments, or have an apathetic attitude toward their academics will inevitably short change their education, their long-term productivity, and their ultimate contributions to this world. And how do the choices we make impact the world around us? If we take it easy, coast, and get by, does this just impact ourselves? If we work hard and do our best in our educational opportunities, what outcomes are possible? Would our impact on the world around us be any different?

Personal Story: I was labeled an over achiever by my friends growing up. Not being very athletic as a youth, I hung around some really smart kids. They would always do better than me on the standardized tests (SAT, ACT, etc.) but somehow I kept up with them in the class room. How? Not being distracted with a lot of extracurricular activities, I focused and worked hard in school and *with the help of my family and classmates* developed consistent, dependable study habits that served me well in college, my career, and throughout my life.

> "The fear of the LORD is the beginning of knowledge..."
>
> Proverbs 1:7a

(c) Financial Success: What significant financially successful person or business ever occurred just by random chance? Was it a roll of the dice or a winning ticket? Didn't it involve effort, study, understanding of the needs of others, creativity, preparation, diligence, hard work, sacrifice, the risk of an upfront investment, and consistency over a long period of time? Sounds like a lot of work! Exactly, life is not easy; it takes effort! Sure there are a select few that win the jackpot. But that is not financial success; that is merely *redistribution of wealth*. What did the winner create or produce for the world? Absolutely nothing, other than moving money from one bank account to another. Yes, there is now a nice sum of money for that individual and perhaps a few select loved ones to enjoy. And yes, perhaps the lucky winner will be generous with the winnings and make the world better. But for the large part, winning lotteries or gambling on financial success is merely personal wealth at the expense of others. No service is provided, no goods are manufactured, no food is grown, no medical diagnosis or treatments are given; it is simply money trading places. If you are counting on a "quick hit" to make your fortune, retire, and live the easy life, then you've bought into the falsehood that life can be easy. It's just not true. We need basics to survive: food, shelter, and clothing. Of course our modern society has many other "necessities" that we all have gotten very accustomed to such as cell phones, computers, and air conditioning! The point is that it takes effort to provide these things plus many other conveniences that make life better for us all. Who is going to provide those things?

True financial success is not solely about individual gain, it's about providing for the needs of those around you. The better you are at fulfilling the needs of others, the more valuable your contributions become, and the more you are compensated for it.

Pretty "simple", just "not easy"! The choice is yours and so are the consequences. You can subscribe to the "get rich quick and coast" approach or you can accept the truth that financial success is a result of sustained effort over a long period of time. I challenge you to consider the potential outcomes of these two approaches to life and the impacts on the world around you.

Personal Story: I had a hole in my pocket as a youth. Give me money, and it was quickly spent on my wants: candy, video games, or cheap toys that didn't last. I had nothing to show for it but brief periods of enjoyment and then a desire for more. It wasn't until I began to learn that life was not all about me but about serving the Lord and others, I took my focus off of my wants and sought to fulfill the needs of others. It's amazing how (1) your ability to help others grows, increasing your value to those around you and (2) your spending patterns change allowing you to spend less than you make and over time have even greater financial ability to help others.

> "He who steals must steal no longer; but rather he must labor, performing with his own hands what is good, so that he will have something to share with one who has need." Ephesians 4:28

(d) Relationships: We'll be discussing relationships a lot because *this is really what life is all about.* So who is/are your closest family members or friends? Who do you trust the most?

Who do you want to spend time with regularly? So how did this relationship come to be? Did it just appear overnight? Was it the outcome a passing glance or smile? Did you just decide one day to have a good relationship and it magically happened? Of course not!

Strong relationships occur when we share life together both the ups and the downs, understand and fulfill each other's needs, sacrifice, achieve and experience defeat together, take risks together, laugh and cry together, *over a long period of time*.

"Rejoice with those who rejoice, and weep with those who weep." Romans 12:15

Strong relationships do not happen overnight. They take sacrifice, compromise, and commitment. They take a selfless attitude. Strong relationships are deeply rooted in trust, and trust is not something that can be bought or lucked into on a roll of the dice. **There is no "easiness" in trust.**

Trust is "simple": it's the outcome of sustained, long-term, constructive behavior towards another that continues to deepen as time passes. It is putting the other person first, giving of yourself, to be willing to go that extra mile for your loved one.

And let me make a very important point; one I hope you will embrace and remember forever:

14

Nothing of importance or value in your life will ever be accomplished on your own.

Please read that again and ponder it. Think about it. Not one accomplishment that you or I will ever be associated with can be done by you and you alone. Name an accomplishment that did not involve the help, assistance, training, provision, instruction, protection, support, and / or encouragement of someone else? The fact that you survived birth proves my point. So what did you do up until the time you where born? Who carried you around for 9 months? Who delivered you? Who fed you, clothed you and changed your stinky diapers, took care of you when you were sick, taught you important life skills and lessons, educated you, gave you opportunities, protected you, etc.? You name anyone that you believe is successful, and I'll guarantee you that they were helped by many, many people along the way.

> "Two are better than one because they have a good return for their labor. For if either of them falls, the one will lift up his companion. But woe to the one who falls when there is not another to lift him up. Furthermore, if two lie down together they keep warm, but how can one be warm alone? And if one can overpower him who is alone, two can resist him. A cord of three strands is not quickly torn apart." Ecclesiastes 4:9-12

Do you have any close relationships in your life? If so, congratulations because you have invested, sacrificed, and intentionally worked hard at it. If not, there is hope. A lot depends on you and your willingness to embrace the "simple" truths of strong relationships and put in the "not easy" efforts to develop and nurture your relationships for the long-term. I'll add that relationships are the most important thing you have in life, and the most influential on what you will be able to accomplish.

> "Teacher, which is the great commandment in the Law?" And He said to him, " 'YOU SHALL LOVE THE LORD YOUR GOD WITH ALL YOUR HEART, AND WITH ALL YOUR SOUL, AND WITH ALL YOUR MIND. This is the great and foremost commandment. The second is like it, 'YOU SHALL LOVE YOUR NEIGHBOR AS YOURSELF.' On these two commandments depend the whole Law and the Prophets." Jesus Christ Matthew 22:36-39

My personal take on the above scripture? We only have to do two things in life, just two:

(1) Love God and
(2) Love others.

Simple, huh? Perhaps not easy all the time! More on that later.

Motivation 2:
Problem Solving

So in addition to my desire to pass on what I know about the uneasiness of life, I'm very analytical. I like to investigate, study people and situations, and solve problems. Life to me is simply working through a series of problems on a moment to moment basis. For example...

When will I get up (or go to bed)?
What will I wear today?
What do I want to be when I grow up?
Where am I going?
How will I get there?
How fast do I plan to get where I am going?
When I get there what will I do?
Wait a minute...why will I do it in the first place?
Who will I do it with?
Who will I do it for?
How important is it and how hard will I try?
What skills or information do I need and how will I properly prepare?
When will I know I'm finished?
What determines success or failure?
What will I eat? How much? When and how often?
When will I have some free time? What will I do? Who will I do it with? For how long?

Some will say "enough already; you just sucked the fun out of life!" That's not my intention. I could go on and on with more daily challenges but hopefully I've made my point. We all solve problems on a regular basis, whether the problems are emotional, physical, technical, medical, financial, recreational, etc. Solving problems actually adds tremendous *significance* to our lives. And please recognize that we don't always have to solve these problems on our own. We often solve them with the assistance of others or, in other cases, get others to solve the problem for us. In other words, we solve problems in the context of relationships. So as we solve problems together, this adds *relational security* to our lives. However, until you're willing to face the reality that life is not easy, it takes effort on your part and on the part of others to get it right, to resolve all these issues over and over, you will never begin to develop your ability to deal with and handle real life. And if you aren't capable and have not developed your potential as an individual, your life will be full of frustration, struggle, confusion, and ultimately require more effort on your part and/or the lives of those around you. Significance and relational security will be an elusive commodity. Why is that important? Read on and you'll see that these two things, *significance and relational security*, are very important to all of us.

We are constantly facing and solving problems, or if you prefer, challenges or opportunities. It's what we all do on a day by day, moment by moment basis. As much as I'd like to relieve you of this truth, I would be doing you a disservice.

Life is not easy! It takes intentional effort for it to work properly.

That's the truth and I want you to embrace it. Once you resign to the fact that "life is simple, it's just not easy", you will begin to grow and develop over time the proper perspective, stamina, skills, patience, and endurance to run this marathon they call life with greater simplicity and greater ease...but remember, life will never be easy!

**Motivation 3:
It's a blessing to give**

"I have shown you in every way, by laboring like this, that you must support the weak. And remember the words of the Lord Jesus, that He said, 'It is more blessed to give than to receive.'"   Acts 20:35

I have received a lot of assistance in solving my own problems in life from my loved ones, authority figures, teachers, co-workers, doctors and nurses, as well as from some hands-on experience. Mostly I have been blessed with Truth that comes only from God Almighty, the Lord of all, the Creator and Giver of life. He has been the greatest influence on my ability to discern, to evaluate, to understand, and to solve. I feel it's my turn to share how the Truth of God's Word, the Bible, and the power of His Holy Spirit have manifested themselves in my life and revealed to me the very title of the book…"life is simple, it's just not easy."

Motivation 4:

TO GLORIFY GOD FOR HE IS WORTHY OF ALL OUR PRAISE

This is last but certainly not least. <u>This is ultimately why I wanted to sign up for this project!</u>

GOD GETS ALL THE CREDIT!

He created you. He created me. My children are His children; I just temporarily get the opportunity to steward them into adulthood. All that I am that has any significance or relational value is because of Him. May all glory be to God Almighty! This is just my personal experience dealing with His Truth.

So please verify anything I happen to say against His Word, the Bible, for all authority rests with the Lord.

If you receive anything from this book that helps you or is a blessing to your life, to God be all the glory for it is only by Him and in His power can we live the "simple – not easy" life!

"Therefore, whether you eat or drink, or whatever you do, do all for the glory of God."

I Corinthians 10:31

****

Your Motives?

So what motivates you and why are you reading this book? Are you ready to perhaps get a greater glimpse into the simple-not easiness of life? The principles and messages in the pages ahead are really very simple. However, I must warn you, some will bring a bit of discomfort and

all will require effort on your part.

I can attest that these have all enriched my life and allowed me to mature emotionally, physically, and spiritually. While I can't guarantee a specific outcome or result, I can guarantee that exposure to these truths will enrich you as a person and prepare you for greater days ahead.

Chapter 2: PERSPECTIVE

Half Full or Half Empty?
It's simply a matter of perspective.

Imagine with me a clear glass that contains some water and that this glass represents your life. So let me ask you this: Do you agree or disagree that the glass is always partially full? After all, if your glass is completely empty, then I'd say your life is over; you're done. If you're reading this, then I'd have to argue that you're "not done" yet! Perhaps another way of saying this is that as long as you have the breath of life, you have something to work with.

So let's explore this analogy a bit further. If you'll indulge me, there's always something in your glass. So how full is your glass? If you focus on the empty part, you will get one result. If you focus on the part that is full, you'll get a different result. So what's the difference? Aren't both perspectives valid and necessary? Well if you focus on what's missing, what's empty, what you don't have, then you will experience discouragement, sadness, depression, envy, regret, and basically a pessimistic view on life. However, if you focus on what you have, then you will experience encouragement, happiness, contentment, and an overall optimistic view on life.

For now I am currently referencing our "worldly glass" which is never completely full. There is always something missing. Life is never completely perfect. You or someone in your life is always experiencing something less than perfection which in turn impacts your life and mine. So what's the use? There will always be something missing, something not working out quite right, a relationship that isn't completely harmonious, a physical ache, pain or illness that we are dealing with. Well isn't that uplifting? As you can see, when you focus on what's not right, you will begin to feel a burden, a weight, a depressed mood about life. That is certainly a choice you can make, but one I avoid as much as possible. If you want the most out of life, if you want to be as constructive as possible, then I encourage you to not lose sight of what you do have working for you in life. I'm not saying to ignore what's missing. If you want to improve your life both now and in the future, then you must have a **balanced view** of your entire life. What I am saying is that if you focus on, dwell on, and become obsessed with only the empty side of your life, this negative and unbalanced perspective will ultimately hinder your forward progress.

Now that summarizes things from a worldly perspective. So what about looking at life from a spiritual perspective? Did you know that it is possible to have your spiritual glass overflowing? So how could that be possible? If you have accepted Jesus Christ as your Lord and Savior, then you already have the Holy Spirit "residing" in your heart. I encourage you to focus on Him, dwell on Him, lean on Him, and surrender control to Him. However, if you have not accepted Christ or have no idea what I'm talking about, then I encourage you to do the following:

(1) Read and understand the gospel of Christ; I explain it this way:

Christ died. Christ was buried. Christ rose from the grave. Jesus Christ did this to take upon Himself the sins of the whole world for all time. He did this because no human can ever do enough or sacrifice enough to be made righteous, i.e. sin-free, before a perfect, Holy God. And if we are unable to remove our sin, then we cannot enter into the presence of God. Jesus Christ's sacrifice on the cross paid the penalty for all the bad stuff you or I have ever done. When we accept Him as our Lord and Savior, Jesus cleanses us spiritually of all our unrighteousness and gives us His righteousness, His perfection in return. Jesus is...

"...the way, the truth, and the life. No one comes to the Father except through Me." John 14:6

*__Personal Note:__ So what about me? How do I measure up? **I have a confession to make.** I am a sinful man, capable of sinful things. If I haven't physically committed the sins mentioned in scripture or referenced in this book, I have probably committed them in my heart. And according to God, that makes me a sinner in desperate need of a Savior. And furthermore, I am still capable of committing sins left to myself and my own desires. It is only by the power of the living God, by the power of His Holy Spirit that I am changed day by day into the man God wants me to be.*

When you believe in Christ and receive Him as your Lord and Savior, you are forgiven of all your sin: past, present, and future. As a believer in Christ, God sees you "in Jesus Christ", without sin and made righteous before Almighty God. You might say "this is too good to be true." Exactly! That's why it's called "The Gospel" which translated means "Good News".

(2) Seek out several followers of Christ that you can trust and ask them how Christ has changed their life. Listen and evaluate what is different about their life? How has their relationship with Christ changed them, particularly their heart? Is their life

better or worse? Is there more or less hope in their life? Meaning? Significance? Relational security? Purpose? I challenge you to look beyond success, money, fame, power and consider what is really important: that which endures forever.

(3) Read up on Christ. Some fantastic books that have personally helped me are listed in the back under "Additional Resources."

If you truly seek, then you will find. And I promise you your life will never be the same.

> "The thief (Satan) comes only to steal and kill and destroy; I came that they may have life, and have it abundantly." Jesus Christ John 10:10

Do you want "abundant" life? You see, when you accept God's grace, His free gift of salvation in Christ, you not only get eternal redemption from all the bad stuff that has gone, is going, or will go on in your life and the promise of an eternal relationship with the God and Creator of the Universe, you immediately receive His Holy Spirit to reside in your heart. Don't believe me? Well perhaps you will believe what God promises in His instruction manual for life, the Bible:

> "I (John the Baptist) baptized you with water; but He (Jesus Christ) will baptize you with the Holy Spirit." Mark 1:8

25

> "Or do you not know (believer in Christ) that your
> body is a temple of the Holy Spirit who is in you, whom
> you have from God, and that you are not your own?"
>
> I Corinthians 6:19

Think about it, if you accepted Christ as your savior, you have God's Holy Spirit "residing" immediately within your heart. It's the truth! Where ever you go, He goes. And when you choose to allow Him, the Holy Spirit, to live in and through you, you will become full of the Spirit, full of God's Spirit. Your spiritual cup will be over flowing with the Spirit of God. After all, how big is God? How much Spirit can He pour out into your life? Is there a limit? I'd have to say "yes" if you're not surrendered to Him, you are full of yourself, and not allowing Him to steer your life. When you or I are in control, we're operating in our own limited power and ability.

To have unlimited power at your disposal, you must surrender and let the Holy Spirit freely flow out of you as you live your life for God and others.

To use an analogy, the Holy Spirit is like a never ending super charged battery that gets even more powerful the more it is used in our life, and it can't be used until we get ourselves out of the way! Think about it another way. We have to become broken, in order for the Holy Spirit to radiate out from us and our life. If we are completely intact in self, operating in our own power, in our own strength, and in our own authority, then we essentially bottle up the Holy Spirit if we are fortunate enough to have Him in the first place.   Let Him in and then allow Him to over flow from your life.

What I'm writing about in the pages ahead is simply God's Truth. If you don't believe me, read about God, the Father, Son, and Holy Spirit, in God's Word, the Bible.

Speaking of the Bible, a pastor friend of mine, Boyd Baker, shared the following which gives a bit on insight into what you can expect from the Bible:

> This book contains the mind of God, the state of man, the way of salvation, the doom of sinners, and the happiness of believers. It's doctrines are holy, its precepts are binding, its histories are true, and its decisions are immutable.   Read it to be wise, believe it to be safe, and practice it to be holy. It contains light to direct you, food to support you, and comfort to cheer you. It is the traveler's map, the pilgrim's staff, the pilot's compass, the soldier's sword, and the Christian's character. Here paradise is restored, heaven opened, and the gates of hell disclosed.   Christ is its grand object, our good its design, and the glory of God its end. It should fill the memory, rule the heart, and guide the feet. Read it slowly, frequently, prayerfully. It is a mine of wealth, a paradise of glory, and a river of pleasure. It is given to you in life, will be opened in the judgment, and be remembered forever.   It

involves the highest responsibility, will reward the greatest labor, and will condemn all who trifle with its sacred contents. *(Author Unknown)*

A life surrendered to Christ, submitted to the will of the Father, and controlled by His Holy Spirit will be fueled by God's Spirit to live a very simple, although not necessarily easy approach to life. I must confess that without this divine power, it will be difficult if not impossible for you or I to understand and embrace the truths I am about to share. Before you read on and if you haven't already, please deal with the following very important question:

Who do you say Jesus is?

The answer to this question is one of the following:

    a) a liar
    b) a lunatic
    c) Lord

Why do I say that? Jesus made numerous bold claims about Himself, perhaps one most notable:

> Jesus said to him, "I am the way, the truth, and the life. No one comes to the Father except through Me."
> John 14:6

Really? This is a rather exclusive statement. Can this statement be partially true? Can other religions reconcile with this verse? I don't see how; it's either true or false. So what if it is not true? Then one must conclude that a) Jesus is not always truthful, in this case he lied, and thus what He says cannot be trusted. Or b) Jesus is a lunatic. After all, who would run around pretending to be God, the promised Messiah of the Old Testament, frustrating the Jewish religious leaders at the time to the point of being accused, ridiculed, humiliated, tortured, and ultimately suffer an excruciatingly painful death on the cross? That wouldn't make any sense at all unless Jesus was simply crazy. If you lean towards either of these first two answers, I encourage you to consider the vast evidence of His life, how He lived, what He said, how He loved, who He lived for, who He died for, what impact He had on multitudes of physically sick people, what impact He had on His disciples, how His disciples behaved before and after His resurrection, and the 100's of prophecies that were fulfilled in His life.

Please don't avoid this very important question
and please make an informed, prayerful decision!

So what if this statement is true? Then one must conclude that **Jesus is who He says He is: He is the promised Messiah. He is Lord. He is The Way. He is The Truth. He is The Life. No one is going to be with God the Father except through Him**. And if He is Lord, then the follow up question for you and me is the following:

Is Jesus your Lord?

You can **know** about Jesus, but that is not the same as **receiving** Jesus. If you haven't dealt with this very important issue in your life, please deal with it now. A good friend of mine put it this way...

> "All around the world, mankind will spend anywhere from 40 to 90 hours a week working to provide food, shelter, and clothing for a week or two, but most of mankind won't spend two days evaluating their eternal condition. I can not understand it. At least make a decision. Is there a life beyond this physical one here on earth? If you say no, chase what this world has to offer, best wishes! I pray you have chosen wisely. If you say maybe or yes, invest the time to seek an answer on how to find it. I did and am convinced that through a God-man, who is the Son of God, named Jesus Christ, my eternity is secured."
> *(Karl Kurz, former COO of Anadarko Petroleum Company)*

So what's it going to be for you? Is your life going to be half empty or half full? <u>My prayer is that you won't settle for either.</u> I pray instead that you seek the One who can give you so much more...

> "...but I came that they may have life, and have it abundantly. "   Jesus Christ   John 10:10b

Chapter 3: PRIORITIES

I. Relationships

"Do not store up for yourselves treasures on earth, where moth and rust destroy, and where thieves break in and steal. But store up for yourselves treasures in heaven, where neither moth nor rust destroys, and where thieves do not break in or steal; for where your treasure is, there your heart will be also."   Jesus Christ   Matthew 6:19-21

What is the one thing that moth and rust cannot destroy? Everything else will disappear from our lives accept for that which moth and rust cannot destroy.   What is it? Where can your heart find true connection?

It is in relationships with God and others.

What can you count on when life is difficult? Do you count on yourself alone? What about the weather? How about the stock market? Your job? Your finances? What about your health? Your spouse or close family member? When the chips are down, when you've been dealt a bad hand, when life just isn't going smoothly, where can you turn for help? I pray you have some close, trustworthy, loving relationships in your life. **I pray even more that you have a personal relationship with the Lord God Almighty through His Son, Jesus Christ.** If not, I encourage you to re-read Chapter 2 and earnestly seek assurance for eternity.

Did you know that everything begins with relationship? Consider the following:

Actions are determined by values.
Values are determined by beliefs.
Beliefs are determined by relationships.
(anonymous)

Do you see that behind all actions are values, then beliefs, then relationships? It all starts with relationships. I've heard in business that the foundation of all accomplishment is relationship. I couldn't agree more. If you disagree, then answer this:

What have you ever accomplished in life without the help of others, without the help of a relationship with someone else?

I'd argue that no one has ever accomplished anything of any significance on their own. We accomplish, discover, triumph, construct, overcome, and complete in the context of relationships.

Behind all actions are ultimately relationships that underpin, encourage, strengthen, guide, and prioritize our behaviors.

If that is so, then how important are the relationships in our life? I would say they are vitally important! So who or what do you relate to? What relationships mold your beliefs and values that ultimately determine your actions? Some relationships that have been very influential in my life include my parents, spouse, grand parents, siblings, in-laws, children, close friends, church family members, teachers, coaches, neighbors, doctors, nurses, co-workers, and bosses. I'd take a serious look into the relationships in your life today and then look forward. Where are these relationships taking you? Are they constructive? Do they have your best interests and the interests of others at heart? Are they self or others-serving? What about God? Is He in the picture? You ultimately have three choices on where you will find your "final answers" in life: God, Others, or Self. So who do you think has the correct answers? Could it be the One who created it all in the first place? Or is it a trusted friend? Or perhaps you know what's best yourself? How will you know? I'd encourage you to study the world around you as objectively as possible. <u>Leave emotion out of it as feelings come and go.</u> Where does wisdom come from? Truth? Love? Deep down we all want these things but…

are we willing to develop the right relationships in order to find them?

"For the LORD gives wisdom; From His mouth come knowledge and understanding."　　　Proverbs 2:6

"The fear of the LORD is the instruction for wisdom, And before honor comes humility."　　Proverbs 15:33

"But if any of you lacks wisdom, let him ask of God, who gives to all generously and without reproach, and it will be given to him."　　　　　James 1:5

"As My Father love Me, I also have loved you; abide in My love. If you keep My commandments, you will abide in My love, just as I have kept My Father's commandments, and abide in His love. These things I (Jesus Christ) have spoken to you that My joy may remain in you and that your joy may be full. This is My commandment, that you love one another as I have loved you."　　　Jesus Christ　　　John 15: 9-12

"Whoever confesses that Jesus is the Son of God, God abides in him, and he in God. And we have known and believed the love that God has for us. God is love, and he who abides in love abides in God, and God in him."

1 John 4:15-16

"The Lord your God in your midst, The Mighty One, will save; He will rejoice over you with gladness, He will quiet you with His love, He will rejoice over you with singing."   Zephaniah 3:17

Obviously I have my view on the subject. God wishes to pour Himself into the hearts and minds of His children, to give them His richest blessings if they will earnestly seek Him. I can say with confidence that God has never, I repeat, never let me down. Have things always gone MY WAY in a particular circumstance?...No. Does that mean God isn't there, that He doesn't care, that He has let me down? At times in my life I might have answered yes. However, as I have grown and matured, I've come to realize that:

Only God knows what's in the future, how everything fits together, how circumstances and events prepare us for a future that only He can see, what the final outcome will be long-term, and how He will use circumstances for eternal good.

Yes, there will be ups and downs in life and yes, at times it will be very difficult to see how this turn out for the best? The truth is that if you love God and are seeking His will, whatever you put in God's hands will ultimately turn out for good. Don't believe me? Well it's a promise from God Himself:

> "And we know that God causes all things to work together for good to those who love God, to those who are called according to His purpose."   Romans 8:28

If you (1) <u>love God</u> and (2) are <u>called according to His purpose</u>, then God promises to work <u>all things</u> for good. Does that mean you will get the outcome you want when you want it...no! Let's unpack this a bit further. Notice the if / then in this verse: <u>if</u> you have a relationship with God (love Him and are called to His purpose), <u>then</u> from this relationship you will receive a promise: when we place our circumstances, our talents, our relationships with spouses, children, friends, etc., our very lives into God's hands, He promises to ultimately use our lives for good. And if all things turn out for ultimate good, that results in tremendous   RELATIONAL   SECURITY   and SIGNIFICANCE in our lives.

Pretty "simple"! The "not easy" part is <u>patiently trusting</u> God through the frustration, difficultly, pain, suffering, and stress during the "downs" in life. And <u>God may ultimately turn it into good long after you and I are no longer around</u>. After all, God is eternal and is working all towards <u>eternal good</u>.

I can testify that God has seen me through many difficulties in life: my father passing when I was 4 years old, a weight problem as a child, inferiority/insecurity complex as a young adult, 9 broken bones at various points in my life including a dislocated wrist, a concussion from a skiing accident, several car accidents, multiple eye surgeries, appendicitis, financial and job uncertainties throughout my career, having two children with heart defects including our first born requiring open heart surgery at 2 days old, caring for my mom during her senior years as her health declined, and most recently my wife Debbie battling stage 3 breast cancer. I don't know how these trials compare to your life, and I'd encourage us not to compete for the worst trials in life. What I do know is that through each of these trials, when I placed each situation into the Lord's hands, He and I worked through them together, and He has used each one to grow our RELATIONSHIP and allow me to experience RELATIONAL SECURITY and SIGNIFICANCE through perseverance and maturing in my abilities and strength to handle life. He has also used all of this to positively impact others around me, i.e. for ultimate good. And I believe He will continue to do so as long as I trust, seek, and follow Him.

"Consider it all joy, my brethren, when you encounter various trials, knowing that the testing of your faith produces endurance. And let endurance have its perfect result, so that you may be perfect and complete, lacking in nothing. " James 1:2-4

> "So I say to you, ask, and it will be given to you; seek, and you will find; knock, and it will be opened to you."
>
> Jesus Christ   Luke 11:9

If you truly seek God, you will find that God is all about relationships. His ultimate goal is that none should perish but have everlasting life with Him for all eternity.

> "For God so loved the world, that He gave His only begotten Son, that whoever believes in Him shall not perish, but have eternal life. For God did not send the Son into the world to judge the world, but that the world might be saved through Him."
>
> Jesus Christ   John 3:16-17

Sounds to me from reading all these scriptures that God wants <u>all to come into a personal relationship with Him.</u> I pray you will seek God and get to know Him. He is amazing! You won't be disappointed!

Let's face it. Good relationships encourage, create, produce, grow, and bless. Bad relationships criticize, destroy, consume, drain, and curse. Which type of relationship do you want to receive? Which type of relationship do you want to give to others?

****

On a side note...I highly recommend an outstanding book by Dr. Henry Cloud and Dr. John Townsend entitled *Boundaries: Face to Face.* It is a must read, trust me. Do you want healthy boundaries in your relationships with friends, parents, spouses, employers, etc. Healthy boundaries are necessary to keep your relationships on a constructive, life-giving course.

Another topic I suggest you investigate is personalities. A study on personalities should be mandatory for everyone. No two people are alike, but we all share similarities in our tendencies and our personality traits. Do you want to understand why some people are easy to get along with while others are just plain difficult? I've listed several resources in the back that have prepared me to develop, protect, and strengthen good relationships. Give one of these books a try and see if you aren't better prepared to face the interesting, sometimes frustrating, but never dull diversity of personalities you will eventually deal with in life. It will help your understanding of others, your communication, and your sanity!

II. The J-O-Y Principal

If you are like me and most everyone I know, we spend a lot of time striving to be happy, happy in our relationships and families, our schools and occupations, and our personal interests and hobbies. Yes, happiness is nice. It feels good to be happy, to be in a "happy place" if you will. But what I have discovered is that perpetual happiness is not possible. In fact, it's impossible. Let me explain. What is the opposite of happiness? Most will agree that sadness comes to mind. OK, so how do you know what happiness feels like if you haven't experienced sadness? Don't you have to go through periods of sadness in order to appreciate the happy times in your life? Now I'm not saying we shouldn't work towards a happy outcome and that it's wrong to be happy. Happiness is a good thing. What I am saying is that…

it's unrealistic to expect to be happy all the time.

There are lots of other examples that demonstrate the opposites or extremes we experience in life:

- In order to appreciate food, you must experience hunger
- In order to appreciate good health, you must have experienced illness or injury
- In order to appreciate warmth, you must experience cold (and visa versa)
- In order to appreciate rest, you must be weary or tired
- In order to appreciate time-off / vacation, you must have worked (at school or your job)
- In order to appreciate freedom, you must have experienced some form of restriction
- In order to appreciate having money or wealth, you must experience being without
- In order to appreciate victory, you must experience defeat

The Bible says it this way:

"To every thing there is a season, and a time to every
purpose under the heaven:
A time to be born, and a time to die;
A time to plant, and a time to pluck up that which is
planted;
A time to kill, and a time to heal;
A time to break down, and a time to build up;
A time to weep, and a time to laugh;
A time to mourn, and a time to dance;
A time to cast away stones, and a time to gather stones
together;
A time to embrace, and a time to refrain from
embracing;
A time to get, and a time to lose;
A time to keep, and a time to cast away;
A time to rend, and a time to sew;
A time to keep silence, and a time to speak;
A time to love, and a time to hate;
A time of war, and a time of peace."

                                    Ecclesiastes 3:1-9

You hopefully get the idea that life has this constant ebb
and flow of "having" and "not having". I'll say this again,
it's unrealistic to live your whole life happy, well fed,
healthy, comfortable, well rested, having time-off for your
personal interests, with plenty of wealth, and in a state of
constant victory. It may sound grand, but it's not reality!

So how does all this relate to J-O-Y? Well I've discovered
that when you accept the whole package that life has to
offer, the ups and the downs, the positives and the

negatives, the good times and the bad, that you begin to be "joy-full" about all that this life has to offer.

Joy to me is accepting life in total and not just one side or the other.

Joy to me is not dependent on our external circumstances, our health, or our emotions. Joy is accepting and being content with life's total package. When we do this, joy becomes a perpetual state that has no end.

Now this all sounds great, but how can I get there from here? This perspective in my opinion is only possible when we have an <u>eternal perspective on life</u>. And this perspective can only come from God Himself. When asked "What was the greatest commandment?" the Lord Jesus replied:

> And He said to him, " 'YOU SHALL LOVE THE LORD YOUR GOD WITH ALL YOUR HEART, AND WITH ALL YOUR SOUL, AND WITH ALL YOUR MIND.' This is the great and foremost commandment. The second is like it, 'YOU SHALL LOVE YOUR NEIGHBOR AS YOURSELF.' "
>
> Jesus Christ   Matthew 22:37-39

Do you see it? Do you see J-O-Y? The first and greatest commandment is to love God, **J**esus. The second commandment is to love your neighbor, **O**ther people that have been placed in your life. So what's left after **J**esus and **O**thers? **Y**ou!

We can have J-O-Y in life only when we put...

<u>J</u>esus (God) first, <u>O</u>thers second, and <u>Y</u>ourself last.

"But seek first His kingdom and His righteousness, and all these things will be added to you. "
                    Jesus Christ   Matthew 6:33

This is the biggest key to discovering the "simple but not easy" life. It is how a yoke, an instrument of work, can become easy and a burden, a responsibility or difficult task, can become light.

"Come to Me, all who are weary and heavy-laden, and I will give you rest. Take My yoke upon you and learn from Me, for I am gentle and humble in heart, and YOU WILL FIND REST FOR YOUR SOULS. For My yoke is easy and My burden is light."
                    Jesus Christ   Matthew 11:28-30

Think about it. If you choose to seek Jesus first, then He through the power of His Holy Spirit will provide, equip, strengthen, guide, and sustain you through life. If you put others second, then you will take your focus off yourself, off "me-myself-and-I", off the difficulties in your own life, off the things missing in your life, off the "half-emptiness" of your life, and you will partner with others to collectively

43

solve the problems in your life. I will say that you still need to put yourself in your priority list as well, just not near the top! You have needs that should be met. <u>Notice I said "needs" and not "wants". There is a big difference.</u> We all "need" certain things to stay healthy physically, emotionally, and spiritually. After all, if you do not take care of yourself, then you will eventually wear yourself out and become a burden on others. No thank you!

> "And my God shall supply all your needs according to His riches in glory by Christ Jesus."   Philippians 4:19

So let's get back to J-O-Y. If you choose to reverse this order, to put yourself and/or others first, then you will, spiritually speaking, be without the Divine help of God, the Lord Jesus Christ, and the Holy Spirit. You will not have His provision, power, wisdom, and perseverance to endure the inevitable difficulties of life. You will not be empowered to "love your neighbor as yourself." The result? I predict a lack of joy, wisdom and discernment, the complexity in your life to increase, the uneasiness and stress in your life to grow, the tension and strain upon your relationships to build, and the difficulty of life to steadily increase as you go at it alone and in your own power. I urge you to consider a different approach. If you don't know God, if you have not been introduced to His Son Jesus, then I urge you to seek Him. His word promises that those who *earnestly* seek will find. And oh what immeasurable blessings you will find!

"So I say to you, ask, and it will be given to you; seek, and you will find; knock, and it will be opened to you. For everyone who asks, receives; and he who seeks, finds; and to him who knocks, it will be opened."
Jesus Christ   Luke 11:9-10

The "simple" part is that this all boils down to a choice, your choice. What will the priorities in your life be? The "not easy" part is where there will be daily, moment by moment effort on your part to **get yourself out of the way, and put God first and others second.** Please, please, please don't miss this very simple yet extremely powerful truth:

You must get yourself out of the way, and put God first and others second.

And when you do (get yourself out of the way that is), watch and see how **abundant**, how **blessed**, how **fulfilling**, and how **purposeful** your life will become!

So how about an analogy to demonstrate this point...

The Snow Ball Analogy

Did you know that you have a seemingly small, insignificant snow ball at the top of a very steep hill covered with snow? You didn't. Well you do. And each and every day you decide which way to push it. You can push it towards one side of the hill or the other. First of all

45

notice that there is effort on your part. You do have to "push" in one direction or the other. The "pushing" represents the "not easiness of life." Regardless of your choice you will have to exert some effort, like it or not. "So what's the difference?" Well there's actually no difference and a huge difference at the same time:

No difference: Well like I said before, there is effort, pushing if you will, either way. And as you push the snow ball, it rolls down one side of the hill, gradually gains speed and gets bigger until it reaches the bottom, and then collides into whatever it comes in contact with. Similarly, if you push it the other direction, the exact same thing happens. It gradually gains momentum and size as it rolls down the slope and then collides into whatever it comes in contact with. OK, same outcome, right? Wrong! There's a big difference in the result at the bottom of the hill. "So what's the difference?"

Difference: It is very different…gigantically different. If you push the snowball towards "God", then you will crash all the things in column A into other people and situations in your life. In contrast, if you push the ball towards "Self", then you will crash all the things listed in column B into other people and situations in your life.

Reflect on the two columns in the following chart:

Column A: God / Others	Column B: Self (i.e. You)
Serving Others	Self Serving
Considerate	Inconsiderate
Wise	Foolish
Complimentary	Critical
Encouraging	Judgmental
Unconditionally Loving	Conditionally Loving
Joyful	Fair weather
Peaceful	Tense, Stressful
Patient	Impatient
Kind	Unkind
Faithful, trustworthy	Untrustworthy
Gentle	Harsh
Self Controlled	Reckless
Constructive	Destructive
Generous	Greedy
Truthful	Deceptive
Over comer; Opportunist	Victim; Complainer
Humble	Arrogant
Concerned	Worried
Hopeful	Gloomy
Caring	Apathetic
Understanding	Disinterested
Compassionate	Mean
Polite	Rude
Helpful	Useless
Live by the Spirit	Live by the flesh

"I have been crucified with Christ; it is no longer I who live, but Christ lives in me; and the life which I now live in the flesh I live by faith in the Son of God, who loved me and gave Himself for me."   Galatians 2:20

"For it is God who works in you both to will and to do for His good pleasure."   Philippians 2:13

So when you come in contact with others, when you come crashing in on another person's life, what kind of snow ball do you want to be? Perhaps said another way...

What kind of snow balls do you want crashing into your life?

Realize one very important point in all this. It all starts with an initial push. Not by your circumstances, not by someone else, not by chance. It all starts with a deliberate action on your part. Let me repeat that.

It all starts with a deliberate decision or action on your part...

to start the ball rolling. And once it starts, it normally gains momentum and grows until it is a mature snow ball headed to impact the world around you. You can stop a snow ball from reaching the bottom; however, that requires significant effort on your part as well as on others. If you push the snow ball in the wrong direction, the longer you let it roll down the hill, complexity creeps into your life, it is anything but simple, and you greatly increase the "not easiness" of life. However, if you choose to push your snow ball in a more selfless, constructive, God-centered direction, you can roll with it; you can gently nudge it along the way, and not ever have to work at redirecting it back up hill and down the other side. And although life still requires constant effort, it becomes much simpler and easier (remember, it's never easy...just easier) as you progress through life.

So what's it going to be? Which way are you going to push? The truth is you have the opportunity to choose which direction to start, but to truly impact others in a constructive fashion over a life time, you need to have J-O-Y in your life. The question is, are you ready for the consequences of your decision; a decision that will impact the rest of your life?

Now I know what some of you are saying: "I'm a good person and exhibit many of the characteristics listed in Column A, but I don't put God first, and I'm not a Christian for that matter." To begin with, consider the following statement made by Jesus Himself:

> "This is the judgment, that the Light has come into the world, and men loved the darkness rather than the Light, for their deeds were evil. For everyone who does evil hates the Light, and does not come to the Light for fear that his deeds will be exposed."
> Jesus Christ   John 3:19-20

49

According to these verses, these words spoken by Jesus Christ Himself, we have two choices: Light (Jesus/God) or Darkness (Evil). Simple, just not easy to embrace.

Also consider John 3:19-20 mentioned previously. This is a very bold, exclusive statement. It's either true or it's not. Am I saying that if you don't put God first then you will automatically do things in Column B? No, that's not what I'm saying. There are many *"relatively good"* people in the world that are not followers of Christ. Those people typically put others before themselves. The question is why? What is their motivation? I can't answer that specifically for everyone, but there will be some motivation behind their actions. The next question to ask is in whose power are they able to live for others? Some practice religions that teach "good works." The challenge with other belief systems - or if you just happen to be a selfless person - is that you must act in your own power and your final outcome is typically resting on your ability to carry out these acts of "good works." My point is that if you are a non-believer in Jesus Christ, you may do good things but ultimately you are doing them for what you gain either personally or what your religion promises you as a reward and thus are ultimately operating for self...

**Your actions are conditional
based upon an outcome.**

To live **continually** in Column A, **unconditionally glorifying God no matter the circumstances**, you must tap into a power source that is unlimited and never ending, the Holy Spirit of the Living God! To do this requires an admission that you and I cannot do this on our own. We need supernatural power that comes only from God. The Lord Jesus Himself said it best:

> "Abide in Me, and I in you. As the branch cannot bear fruit of itself, unless it abides in the vine, neither can you, unless you abide in Me. I am the vine, you are the branches. He who abides in Me, and I in him, bears much fruit; **for without Me you can do nothing**."
>
> Jesus Christ   John 15:4-5

Oh, and one final thought…

> **"Every person has the power to make others happy.**
> **Some do it simply by entering a room –**
> **Others by leaving the room."**
>
> William Arthur Ward, author

So what kind of person do you want to be?

III. Forgiveness

Have you ever had to offer your forgiveness to someone that you have hurt? Have you ever had to receive forgiveness from some who has hurt you? Forgiveness is a 2 step process. It involves **offering** and **receiving**. Either step can be done individually to **provide freedom to live your life** independent of issues that cause separation in your relationships. However, <u>both must occur</u> in order for forgiveness to be complete and to **restore** relationships. Offering forgiveness and receiving forgiveness are two different things done by two separate persons:

Offering Forgiveness is for the one offended; it is a gift offered to the one at fault in order to receive their gift of repentance

Receiving Forgiveness is for the one at fault; it is "repentance" offered to the one offended in order to receive their gift of forgiveness

Repentance, by the way, is admitting you were wrong and doing your best to change your behavior and not make the same mistake in the future.

Restoration between the one offended and the one at fault <u>can only occur when both of these conditions are satisfied.</u>

So how about an example? I'll use myself as the one at fault and my wife, Debbie, as the one offended since that is perhaps the most obvious, realistic, most often, real life scenario I can come up with! So before we go into our options, let's discuss the terms above in more detail.

So what does it mean to "**offer forgiveness**"? It means to cancel the debt the other person owes you. And once you offer the other person this gift, what does that do for you?

Well for one, it releases you from any anxiety, bitterness, grudge, hatred, anger, revenge, or similar destructive emotions that you might feel towards the other person. By you "forgiving" your neighbor, you are now free from whatever it was that created a separation between the two of you. But to be clear, this does not **restore the relationship**, at least not yet. The opposite of offering forgiveness is to be unforgiving, maintain a grudge, and withhold forgiveness until the one at fault apologizes.

So what does it mean to "**receive forgiveness**"? It begins with an admission that you were wrong and a desire to seek the other person's forgiveness, to apologize, and finally repent. To "repent" is to change your behavior away from that which was separating the relationship. It is a gift you offer the person that was wronged. It is seeking to pay your debt. And once you offer the other person this gift of repentance, what does that do for you? Well for one, it releases you from any guilt, anxiety, bitterness, grudge, hatred, anger, revenge, or similar destructive emotion that you might feel towards the other person. By repenting towards your neighbor, you are now free from whatever it was that created a separation between the two of you. But to be clear, this does not necessarily **restore the relationship**, at least not yet. The opposite is to be "unrepentant" and maintain that you are right and other person is wrong.

Restoration of the relationship occurs only when forgiveness <u>offered</u> AND forgiveness <u>received</u> occurs.

So what do these **BEHAVIORS** look like? Let's suppose that I am at fault and have done something to hurt my wife, Debbie. Debbie's options are as follows:

1. She can offer me forgiveness <u>BEFORE</u> I ever seek her forgiveness; or
2. She can wait for me to come to my senses, admit I was wrong, apologize, and in time demonstrate that I have repented, changed my ways, and am sincere about receiving her forgiveness. And <u>AFTERWARDS</u>, offer me her forgiveness; or
3. She can <u>WITHHOLD</u> her forgiveness from me indefinitely

And what about for me, the one at fault:

1. I can admit I was wrong, repent, change my ways, and never offend or hurt Debbie in that manner ever again <u>BEFORE</u> Debbie gives any indication that she's willing to forgive me; or
2. I can wait till Debbie shows a willingness to forgive me and then <u>AFTERWARDS</u> seek her forgiveness by repenting and receiving her forgiveness; or
3. I can justify my behavior, claim Debbie is being unreasonable, not apologize or worse continue to do what ever it was that offended her. In other words I can <u>WITHOLD</u> my repentance from her.

So now let's discuss the **OUTCOMES** of these behaviors. For my spouse, Debbie, the one offended:

Option 1 - <u>guarantees her freedom</u> from the anxiety, frustration, anger, bitterness, revenge, and other destructive emotions surrounding the issue that offended her. She can <u>move on regardless of what I do</u>.

Option 2 - frees her as well but <u>is conditional on what I do</u>. If I don't repent, she is <u>choosing</u> to hold herself hostage to the destructive emotions that accompany the issue until I decide to do the right thing.

Option 3 - <u>guarantees her bondage</u> to the anxiety, frustration, anger, bitterness, revenge, and other destructive emotions surrounding the issue that offended her. She can <u>NEVER move on regardless of what I do</u>.

So what about for me, the one at fault?

Option 1 - <u>guarantees my freedom</u> from the guilt, anxiety, frustration, anger, bitterness, revenge, and other destructive emotions surrounding the issue that offended her. It will hopefully never happen again if I've truly repented, i.e. I'll try my best not to ever do it again! I can <u>move on regardless of what my spouse does</u>.

Option 2 - frees me as well but <u>is conditional on what my spouse does</u>. Only when I'm certain I'll be offered forgiveness will I admit wrong doing, apologize, repent, and accept her forgiveness. Until Debbie offers forgiveness or demonstrates a willingness to forgive, I am choosing to hold myself hostage to the destructive emotions that accompany the issue.

Option 3 - <u>guarantees my bondage</u> to the guilt, anxiety, frustration, anger, bitterness, revenge, and other destructive emotions surrounding the issue that offended her. I can <u>NEVER move on regardless of what Debbie does</u>.

I hope you are getting the point here. Problems in relationships are inevitable, they involve two or more people, and it takes actions on both sides to restore the relationship. You as an individual can take one of three approaches:

1. Unconditional
2. Conditional
3. Selfish

No matter what side of the issue you are on, if you take the **unconditional approach**, you will free yourself from the bondage of unforgiveness and unrepentance, and your relationships will more than likely be restored over and over again. And, if you act independent of the other person, you will more likely…

encourage the other person to respond towards restoration,

whether it is offering or receiving forgiveness. And as this happens over and over, the relationships in your life will grow deeper, stronger, and more intimate. Sounds pretty nice!

If you take the **conditional approach**, you might free yourself; you might not. Until the other person responds in such a way that prompts you in turn to *react* towards restoration, you will remain in bondage and carry around the baggage of what ever it is that is separating your relationship. And what if the other person never responds the way you want them to? Well, that will look a lot like option 3.

I don't believe I need to go into detail how ugly, destructive, and devastating the **selfish approach** would be to our relationship. In fact, after a few episodes there might not be much of a relationship left to salvage!

Do you want others dictating your feelings? Do you want others deciding how strong your relationships will be? Do you want deep, trustworthy, loving, encouraging relationships in your life? I know, "but it's hard to offer or receive forgiveness when the other person just isn't acting properly." Or another one I like: "they don't deserve it!" I know it is **NOT EASY.** But it is **VERY SIMPLE!**

Offering forgiveness is for you, the offended. It is a gift you offer the other person at fault to restore your relationship. But what if they never apologize? What then? That's a great question. You can't control the other person and you shouldn't. Right now I'm talking to you, the offended. We've all been offended from time to time. It's up to you. Do you want to carry around all the baggage of strained relationships or do you want to move on? The choice is yours. When you or I genuinely offer unconditional forgiveness, we are blessed with freedom to move on.

Offering repentance, i.e. seeking to receive forgiveness is for you, the one at fault. It is a gift you offer the person who was wronged by you to restore your relationship. But what if they never offer me their forgiveness? What then? Once again, you can't control the other person, and right now I'm talking to you, the one at fault. Have you ever hurt someone else? Said the wrong thing at the wrong time? Of course! We've all hurt other people in our life, haven't we? No one is perfect. However, when we do hurt others, we can do everything in our power to restore the relationship. The choice is yours. When you or I genuinely repent and seek to receive forgiveness, we are blessed with freedom to move on.

Remember how important relationships are in your life? Remember that nothing of any significance or value is ever accomplished on your own? The process of offering and receiving forgiveness is a beautiful thing in that it actually strengthens relationships if it is done sincerely and within a J-O-Y full approach to life.

So what about the opposite? What if the one who is wronged doesn't offer forgiveness or the one at fault doesn't seek it out through repentance? Well, **what does that say about the importance of the relationship?**

"Resentment is like taking poison and expecting the other person to die."
(Malachy McCourt, Irish-American actor, writer, and politician)

I must add a disclaimer about **consequence** and **trust**. What I've been discussing is <u>restoration of relationships</u> through giving and receiving forgiveness. Even when there is genuine forgiveness offered and forgiveness received,

that doesn't necessarily translate into release of consequences or restoration of trust...

with regard to the other person. I can forgive you for breaking my favorite fishing rod in the car door (restore relationship), however, you may still have to replace it (there still may be a consequence...of course, I could cancel that debt as well!). I can apologize and stop behaving a certain way and demonstrate my repentance (seek to restore the relationship) and you can forgive me (free our relationship from the issue); however, your trust in me may not be restored for a long time if ever.

Trust is conditional based upon a pattern of behavior.

If you want someone to trust you, you must act a certain way consistently over a long period of time. That is why trust is such a valuable yet elusive characteristic in our relationships. Said another way,

There is no such thing as unconditional trust.

"But wait a minute. I offered _____ forgiveness and they said they were sorry, but they keep doing that which annoys or hurts me!" Well, there could be a couple of things going on here.

1. The one at fault (<u>which by the way describes all of us!</u>) is by nature imperfect and prone to mistakes. And even when we genuinely repent and are trying our best to change, mistakes happen, and we can drift back into old habits. Have you ever made the same mistake twice?
2. On the other hand, the one at fault may not be sincere. If someone says one thing and does another, I believe that is called being a hypocrite. Have you ever met anyone like that before?

Actions speak louder than words.

In the first instance, I would say that the one at fault was repentant and did receive your forgiveness. They just need some extra mercy, grace, and perhaps another dose of your forgiveness to work out a fault in their life. However, in the second instance, I would question whether the one at fault ever "received" your forgiveness. And if they haven't received your forgiveness, then the issue that separated the two of you remains for the one at fault, and they remain in bondage to all the baggage associated with that issue. You, the offended, on the other hand can be free emotionally by "offering" them forgiveness. It is up to them to decide whether or not their relationship with you is important or valuable enough to change their behavior and "receive" your forgiveness. Remember...

Repentance is necessary to <u>receive</u> <u>forgiveness</u> and thus <u>become forgiven.</u>

So let's talk a bit about God? How does He handle this issue? Did you know that God freely offers His forgiveness, and He desires that you receive it? He's in the business of "offering forgiveness" and is so full of mercy (not giving us what we deserve) and grace (giving us what we don't deserve) that He sent His Son, Jesus, to pay for all the bad stuff (sin) that you and I do in this life. Words cannot express how wonderful and unconditionally loving God truly is! If you don't believe me, perhaps you would take Him at His word:

"If My people who are called by My name will humble themselves, and pray and seek My face, and turn from their wicked ways, then I will hear from heaven, and will forgive their sin and heal their land."

2 Chronicles 7:14

"Blessed the Lord, O my soul;
And all that is within me, bless His Holy Name!
Bless the Lord, O my soul,
And forget not all His benefits:
Who forgives all your iniquities,
Who heals all your diseases,
Who redeems your life from destruction,
Who crowns you with loving kindness and tender mercies ."

Palms 103:1-4

"And saying, "The time is fulfilled, and the kingdom of God is at hand. Repent and believe in the gospel."

Jesus Christ   Mark 1:15

"For God so loved the world that He gave His only begotten Son, that whoever believe in Him should not perish but have everlasting life. For God did not send His Son into the world to condemn the world, but that the world through Him might be saved. He who believes in Him is not condemned, but he who does not believe is condemned already, because he has not believed in the name of the only begotten Son of God. And this is the condemnation, that the light has come into the world, and men loved the darkness rather than light, because their deeds were evil. For everyone practicing evil hates the light and does not come to the light, lest his deeds should be exposed. But he who does the truth comes to the light, that his deeds may be clearly seen, that they have been done in God."

Jesus Christ   John 3:16-21

"Therefore repent and return, so that your sins may be wiped away, in order that times of refreshing may come from the presence of the Lord; and that He may send Jesus, the Christ appointed for you, whom heaven must receive until the period of restoration of all things about which God spoke by the mouth of His holy prophets from ancient time."

Act 3:19-21

"...that they may receive forgiveness of sins and an inheritance among those who are sanctified by faith in Me."

Jesus Christ   Acts 26:18b

"Therefore, having been justified by faith, we have peace with God through our Lord Jesus Christ, through whom we have access by faith into this grace in which we stand, and rejoice in the hope of the glory of God."

Romans 5:1

"But God demonstrated His own love towards us, in that while we were still sinners, Christ died for us. Much more then, having now been justified by His blood, we shall be saved from wrath through Him. For if when we were enemies we were reconciled to God through the death of His Son, much more, having been reconciled, we shall be saved by His life. And not only that, but we also rejoice in God through our Lord Jesus Christ, through whom we have now received the reconciliation." Romans 5:8-11

"The Lord is not slack concerning His promise, as some count slackness, but is longsuffering toward us, not willing that any should perish but that all should come to repentance." 2 Peter 3:9

Sounds to me from all these scriptures that God is offering us His forgiveness and desires for all to repent and receive. So the key question for you and I is this:

Have we *received* His forgiveness?

I refer you back to Chapter 2 on Perspectives. And once we have received His forgiveness,

what does God expect us to do with regard to forgiveness in our life and in the other relationships in our life?

"And forgive us our debts, as we forgive our debtors." Jesus Christ Matthew 6:12

"For if you forgive men their trespasses, your heavenly Father will also forgive you. But if you do not

64

forgive men their trespasses, neither will your Father forgive your trespasses." Jesus Christ   Matthew 6:14

"Therefore, if you bring your gift to the alter, and there remember that your brother has something against you, leave your gift there before the alter, and go your way. First be reconciled to your brother, and then come and offer your gift." Jesus Christ   Matthew 5:23-24

"Then Peter came to Him and said, 'Lord, how often shall my brother sin against me, and I forgive him? Up to 7 times?' Jesus said to him, 'I do not say to you up to seven times, but up to seventy times seven.'"
Matthew 18:21

"And whenever you stand praying, if you have anything against anyone, forgive him, that your Father in heaven may also forgive you your trespasses.   But if you do not forgive, neither will your Father in heaven forgive your trespasses." Jesus Christ   Mark 11:26

"Let all bitterness, wrath, anger, clamor, and evil speaking be put away from you, with all malice. And be kind to one another, tenderhearted, forgiving one another, even as God in Christ has forgiven you."
Ephesians 4:31-32

"Therefore, as the elect of God, holy and beloved, put on tender mercies, kindness, humility, meekness, longsuffering, bearing with one another, and forgiving one another, if anyone has a complaint against another, even as Christ forgave you, so you also must do. But above all these things, put on love, which is the bond of perfection. And let the peace of God rule in your hearts, to which also you were called in one body; and be thankful. Let the word of Christ dwell in you richly in all wisdom, teaching and admonishing one another in psalms and hymns and spiritual songs, singing with grace in your hearts to the Lord. And whatever you do in word or deed, do all in the name of the Lord Jesus, giving thanks to God the Father through Him."

Colossians 3:12-17

"If possible, so far as it depends on you, be at peace with all men."   Romans 12:18

Sounds to me from all these scriptures that God wants us to practice offering forgiveness to others; over and over again! Let's face it. You and I make mistakes in our relationships. We're going to mess up at some time or another, guaranteed, no matter how hard we try not to. So what's the answer? Read those scriptures again. The answer is VERY SIMPLE...IT'S JUST NOT EASY to do:

1. OFFER FORGIVENESS to those who hurt you, and
2. RECEIVE FORGIVENESS through REPENTANCE
   to those whom you have hurt

I know it's not easy, and it's impossible in our own power.

You must abide in the One who can empower you to do this over and over again. You must humble yourself. In the end it's a choice, your choice. You can be free and promote restoration in all your relationships or you can be in bondage and promote separation in all your relationships. Which side do you want? If you want to restore relationships, I encourage you to always begin with the Lord. Accept His forgiveness, pray for Him to change your heart, and allow Him to empower you to restore the other relationships in your life.

"But seek first the kingdom of God and His righteousness, and all these things shall be added to you." Jesus Christ   Matthew 6:

Chapter 4: Practically Speaking on....

I. Winning

Do you like to lose? I don't. In fact, I can't stand to lose. So I've decided that I won't. That's right, I never lose. You might say that is arrogant on my part, but I invite you to consider the following perspective. If you maximize your ability or your talent, try your best each day and let the results fall where they may, then I would argue that it's impossible for you to lose. I personally define losing as putting forth a poor effort, having a bad attitude, or giving up. Notice I did not say I define losing as making a mistake. We all make mistakes from time to time. No one is perfect. And while results aren't always perfect, your level of effort, your will to always do your best in whatever it is you do, can approach perfection. If you've done all you can, what else is there to do? You gave it all you had. I say you can't *lose* in that situation; you can only be *beaten* by a superior performance from someone else.

So how about a sports analogy? I like to play golf and consider myself a decent golfer given the amount of free time I have to practice and play. Let's just suppose that I had the opportunity to compete against Jack Nicklaus, the winner of more golf majors than anyone in history. I could shoot my best round ever and come up short every time to Jack's mediocre score. Did I *lose* to Jack Nicklaus? Some may say yes, but I say "no way"! I don't' care who I'm competing against, I'm going to try my best every time - whether at work or play - to do as well as I possibly can on that particular day. Day to day my performance will vary but not my level of effort. <u>Losing for me is not an option.</u> Jack may shoot a better score and *defeat* me, you might even say I was *beaten* that day. Fine, but...

I refuse to lose.

I encourage you to eliminate *losing* in your life. If I do my best, I can hold my head high and live in such a way as to never face losing again, not even in a golf match with Jack Nicklaus!

So how about a Biblical analogy? Do you know the story of the talents in Matthew 25:14-30. In this story the master gives 5 talents (the "talents" are coins) to one servant, 3 to another, and 1 to a third. The master expects each servant to be a good steward of what he, the master, has entrusted to each one, to do all they can with what they have been given. The first servant doubles his 5 talents, earns 5 more, and returns 10 to the master. The master replies "well done good and faithful servant." The second servant takes their

3 and earns another 3, also doubling their talents, returning 6 to the master. Again the master replies "well done good and faithful servant." Notice that although the second servant earned less than the first, the response is the same. The master recognized that each servant had different abilities, different "talents" and rewarded each one based on the talents given to each and how well they multiplied their talents. To the first servant who had been given 5 talents, more was expected. How different our world is when it comes to competition. We live in a winner-take-all society. We rarely look at what is behind the outcome to see who truly performed well. In our society, the first servant *won* because they earned 5 while the second servant only earned 3. While this is true, this worldly view does not take into account that we all have different abilities. So what about the third servant, the one that had been given only one talent? Well that servant did not multiply their talent. Rather, they buried it in the sand; they didn't do anything with it and simply returned it to the master **unused and to no one's benefit!** How would you like that written on your tombstone? So what was the master's reply? Well it wasn't pretty. The master expected the third servant to do all they could with what they were given even though it was less than the other servants. The third servant did NOTHING! The master was very disappointed and took the one talent from the third servant and gave it to the first servant who had demonstrated good stewardship. Do you see the connection?

We should not measure ourselves against others; rather we should measure ourselves against what we could have done if we tried our best.

That is the true measure of good stewardship, and if we accomplish our best on any given day, losing is no longer an option!

Ok, I know…"but I don't like to get beaten either!" Fine, healthy competition is good in that it pushes all of us to be the best we can be. I'm all for striving to *win,* and I'm not suggesting you have to like getting beat! My point is as you do your best, i.e. *not lose…*there is *SIGNIFICANCE* and growth towards your ultimate best. In addition, if you are measuring yourself against yourself, you're more likely to compete with integrity, and you're more likely to maintain a *GOOD RELATIONSHIP* towards your opponent. And if you're trying your best with integrity, won't you earn the appreciation and respect of your opponents, coaches, teammates, fans, or coworkers? You can have both *SIGNIFICANCE* and *RELATIONAL SECURITY* **regardless of the outcome** if you approach your competition from a healthy perspective. And always remember, if your opponent wins, congratulate them! If your desire is to do better next time, then use your experience as motivation to train harder for the next opportunity!

II. The Package deal

"You can't have your cake and eat it too."

Have you ever heard this phrase before? There are many, many choices we make in life that define one set of outcomes (fellowship, activities, or consequences) vs. another. To say it a different way, all of us choose one *package* over another all the time. Take the following example:

On Sunday evening you are invited to go to the ball game with some friends or you can stay home and relax. You also know that Monday morning you have to get up early, drive to the airport, and catch the early flight for a very important business meeting. So here's the "package deal"...

Choice	Ball Game Package	Rest and Relaxation Package
Fellowship	with friends	with family prior to leaving town
Activity	entertainment	preparation for trip and rest
Consequence	fun, excitement, grow relationship with friends, less preparation time for business trip, less time for rest	lower key and less excitement, grow relationships with family, better prepared for business trip, well rested

I've been on both sides of similar situations in my life. In this instance, <u>neither choice is necessarily good or bad</u>; it's just a choice depending on what's most important at a particular time in your life. My point is you can't go to the game and stay at home at the same time; that's impossible. You must choose one *package* or another, and you must accept the consequences of your choice. Some more significant "package deals" in life include:

- Who you will marry…your spouse
- College: to go or not to go, where, what major
- Career path, specific job role, employer
- Where you will live
- Home or car purchase
- Your attitude
- Your faith or belief system

There are many, many more, and we make these choices all the time. If we're going to make "package deal" type choices, shouldn't we better understand the details and potential consequences of these packages, think through how this fits within our value system and our desired outcomes? Only then can we make an informed choice, <u>especially when it comes to those major life-changing packages.</u> So what is hopefully simple to understand is that

Life is a "package deal" that we choose constantly.

The not-easy part is…

1. researching, thinking through the details and outcomes relative to our priorities, values, and desires, and **making one informed decision or choice after another**
2. **having to accept the entire package,** the good and the not-so-good parts!

Just about all packages have a bit of both. Hopefully you will select packages where the benefits and blessings out-weigh the costs and challenges. If you choose to work at understanding and selecting these "package deals", then I would argue that more often than not, you will make wise choices and receive the outcomes you desire. However, if you choose to make uninformed decisions with little or no thought about the details, values and consequences, then your odds of having unexpected, unwanted outcomes will increase and greatly complicate your life. You only have one life. I urge you to consider investing a bit of time and energy on those major "package deal" choices that last a lifetime and beyond.

Oh, and once you've made a decision, please accept the *responsibility for your choice* and don't complain or blame others for the *consequences of your choice*!

III. Complaining

The simple, not easy approach?...**Don't complain!** It does not do you or anyone else any good

So what do you complain about? To complain, if you think about it, is rather easy. That, in and of itself, should be a warning. If something is easy, be careful because life isn't! And yes, to not complain, to learn to constructively deal with the frustrations of life is not easy. But if you learn to approach your situations from a more constructive perspective, i.e. avoid complaining, then you will be more prepared, more equipped, more able to deal with and handle the "not easy" situations in your life. So here are a few that seem to creep into my life...

(a) Undesirable outcome in competition – Do you whine and scream when you don't win? Or do you congratulate your opponent and practice or compete harder for the next time? How do you want your opponent to behave if you are the winner? I said earlier that I don't like to *lose* so I don't. I do get *beaten* and to be honest, I'm not too keen on that either. So what do you do if you don't get the outcome you wanted? Complain? I have from time to time, especially when I play cards. It isn't very constructive and has never improved my life! You can't expect to *win* every time. There will be moments in your life that defeat is the reality. Yes there's disappointment and perhaps you weren't at your best that day. Fine. You have a choice: (1) look back and complain or (2) realize that there is another day, learn from your experience, train and practice harder if you want to get better, and look ahead with anticipation to your next opportunity. I refer you back to the section on winning for more thoughts on this subject.

(b) Unfairness – it's a good thing life is not fair…

I can guarantee you that at some point in your life you will be treated *unfairly*. We live in an imperfect world surrounded by imperfect people. Should we strive to be fair? Absolutely. But it is unrealistic to expect to live your life and never experience some unfairness from time to time. So what should you or I do about it? We could complain about it, but I challenge you to consider what good that will do for you and for others around you? I believe a better approach is to seek ways to constructively influence the circumstances to reduce or eliminate any unfairness in our lives. Do all you can to better the situation. And when you're done, make sure you take care of any unforgiveness issues (see section on forgiveness). If you're still tempted to dwell on your situation, just remember how Jesus was treated for teaching wisdom, loving others, healing the sick, speaking truth, serving others, living a sinless life, and subjecting Himself to the greatest example of unfairness in history: to be ridiculed, tortured, humiliated, falsely accused, and ultimately crucified for doing nothing wrong! Perhaps it's a good thing life isn't fair. If life was truly fair, wouldn't it be us on the cross and not Jesus?

(c) Weather – this is outside of our control. I love the following phase...

> **"there's no such thing as bad weather...
> just bad clothing!"**
> *(Scandinavian/Norwegian saying)*

The weather will disappoint you from time to time. Learn to deal with it, and stop making things worse! Life, your particular circumstance, the weather...it happens. **There are things outside our control, but one thing you can control (if you choose to do so) is <u>your response</u> to what happens.** Watch the weather channel and plan accordingly.

(d) Irresponsibility
I'm very guilty of this one! If you are surrounded by irresponsible people, you can (1) focus on them and complain or (2) <u>learn from other's mistakes and accept their gift of showing you what not to do in life.</u> In other words, you can avoid their mishaps. I struggle with this, so you have my sympathies if you're dealing with this issue. Realize that eventually people will reap what they sow in time; be patient, persevere. Yes, it's really very simple...it's just not easy.

(e) Problems
Are you part of the solution or part of the problem? It's either one or the other, and I've been on both sides. I prefer life when everything's running smoothly, when my actions get the results I'm looking for, when my loved ones are happy and prosperous. Isn't it frustrating when

problems arise that shake our world and cause us to expend extra effort to deal with them? We all have problems. It's a universal truth that everyone will deal with problems in life, and we all complain about it, don't we? However,

> *If you're complaining about a problem, then haven't you just become part of that problem?*

And to get right down to it, you're either in one group of people or the other. You're either working to solve problems or you're the opposite: you're working to create or magnify problems. Is the world improving around you or is it getting worse? Perhaps another way to look at it is this:

> *What type of people do you want to hang around with, solvers of problems or creators of problems?*

Now please don't misunderstand, we all need help from each other from time to time as life is full of challenges…remember, it's not easy. And allowing others to help us from time to time is a blessing to all, so by all means help others and get some help along the way. What I am suggesting is to consider whether you are *manufacturing problems* or *working with others to manufacture solutions*. Another way to say this:

Are you a net producer or net consumer? Do you…

Net Producer	Net Consumer
Give	Take
Solve problems, create solutions	Create problems, hinder solutions
Seek opportunities to help others	Expect from others, entitlement mentality
Participate, engage in the race of life	Spectate, sit on the sideline of life
Practice generosity	Seek a handout
Multiply your talents (Matt 25:14-29)	Bury your talents in the ground
Promote growth by "teaching a man to fish"	Promote dependence by "giving a man a fish"
Encourage others with your words (Eph 4:29)	Discourage others with your words

"The desire of the sluggard puts him to death, for his hands refuse to work; all day long he is craving, while the righteous gives and does not hold back."

Proverbs 21:25-26

"For even when we were with you, we used to give you this order: if anyone is not willing to work, then he is not to eat, either. For we hear that some among you are leading an undisciplined life, doing no work at all, but acting like busybodies."

2 Thessalonians 3:10-11

(f) Inconsiderate behavior
Here's another one that I struggle with, especially when I am behind the wheel in rush hour traffic…ouch! Yes, it's extremely frustrating when someone cuts you off or drives in such a way that puts you and others at risk. Do I get upset?…sometimes. Do I verbalize my frustration in a constructive fashion?...not always. As with irresponsible behavior and problems, the same principles apply. Is it easy to deal with these? Not at all, just ask my family! It takes intentional effort, and I believe supernatural power, i.e. the Holy Spirit, to do this consistently over a lifetime. Focus on helping others, model considerate behavior, and take your focus off of the inconsiderate behaviors.

(g) Unkind words
I'll be the first to admit that I'm guilty of having said things in my life that I wish I could take back. The difficulty is that once you've said something, you can never take it back; you can only manage the impact of your words going forward. I'm not too fond of hearing negative, mean, critical, emotionally hurtful things spoken in my presence, whether they are directed to me or not. It tends to bring me down and can draw me into an attitude where I actually participate in it. Yuck! The best thing I've found to do is practice the following advice:

> "And why do you look at the speck in your brother's eye, but do not consider the plank in your own eye? Or how can you say to your brother; 'Let me remove the speck you're your eye'; and look, a plank is in your own eye? Hypocrite! First remove the plank from your own

eye, and then you will see clearly to remove the spec from your brother's eye."

Jesus Christ   Matthew 7:3-5

"Do not let any unwholesome talk come out of your mouth, but only what is useful for building others up according to their needs so that it may benefit those who listen."

Ephesians 4:29

I believe if we would simply follow these two scriptures, a vast majority of the complexities in life would evaporate overnight. What do you think?

Before you speak, make sure your words are consistent with these truths. If not, then silence is a better option!

(h) School

Did I ever complain about school? Sure. Did it help me in life? Not exactly. Do you want to be uneducated, dependent on others, clueless on how to manage life in your adult years, and in general not reach your full potential? That's just not acceptable for me and completely inconsistent with good stewardship. Learning is a necessary part of life. We all must learn to steward our opportunities with excellence, not only for ourselves but for everyone else in our life. **School, education, is a gift, not a punishment!** It will improve our lives if we choose to allow that outcome! Your choice.

(i) Work

Work can be frustrating, and perhaps you're in a job or working for a company that just isn't a good fit for you. You can always make a change. What I challenge you to do is think about the big picture. Do you want others to take care of you, so you can get a free pass, consume, play for a living, and be completely irresponsible as an adult? Is that what you would expect from your co-worker? Spouse? How about your children? If no one works then we all perish! Work is a necessary part of life. If you don't work then someone else will have to do it for you. That sounds like a whole lot more trouble and complexity, i.e. *not easiness*, for those who do decide to work. "But I don't like my work!" That happens from time to time. Stop complaining and seek another job opportunity that is better suited for you. Get re-trained if necessary. Find an occupation, a job that you find significance through fulfilling the needs of others. The rewards will follow if you work to solve problems for others. Consider moving if necessary to find meaningful work that benefits others. And if you add a huge dose of the following, I can guarantee you'll become a more valuable employee...

> "And whatever you do, do it heartily, as to the Lord and not to men, knowing that from the Lord you will receive the reward of the inheritance; for you serve the Lord Christ." Colossians 3:23

In other words...

...work for the Lord
and you will find favor
with God and man!

(j) "What you permit"

I hope you take this one particularly to heart. How many times do people complain about things that they have either allowed or are encouraging to occur in their life? This makes no sense to me, but I see it all the time. People complain about their work but make no effort to get another job or learn a new skill. Students complain about their grades but see no problem skipping assignments or staying up late at night watching TV, playing video games, or socializing on Facebook. Parents complain about their children's behavior but don't lovingly train or discipline them. What about relationships? People complain all the time about how so-in-so treated me, but they do nothing to constructively discuss the issue with the person they are complaining about. Before you complain, please consider if you have contributed to the issue, situation, etc. And if there are some things you can do to improve what ever it is you want to complain about, then by all means take constructive action towards a better outcome. Above all...

"Don't complain about what you permit."
(anonymous)

How about being completely free from complaining? Interested? What if you decided that from now on, you no longer expected anyone to do anything for you or to treat you in any particular manner? What if you lived your life 100% of the time unexpectantly towards the world around you? What would that look like? Well for starters, you would never be disappointed! And to go a step further, wouldn't everything constructive that you received from anyone around you become a gift? After all, if you don't expect anything from anyone, then everything that comes into your life is through a voluntary act by someone else. And if everything that you received was a gift, wouldn't you become more grateful and have nothing to complain about?

Nice try, huh? We all have expectations of others, don't we? But are your expectations reasonable? I challenge you to limit your expectations of others and allow them to freely give, to freely pour into your life *voluntarily and not out of obligation.*

> "Do all things without grumbling or disputing; so that you will prove yourselves to be blameless and innocent, children of God above reproach in the midst of a crooked and perverse generation, among whom you appear as lights in the world..."   Philippians 2:14

> "Do nothing from selfishness or empty conceit, but with humility of mind regard one another as more important than yourselves; do not merely look out for your own personal interests, but also for the interests of others. Have this attitude in yourselves which was also in Christ Jesus,..."   Philippians 2:3-5

A final thought on complaining…

This is a fundamental truth in life that eventually catches up with everyone, and I mean EVERYONE, regardless of their nationality, gender, faith system, social status, political affiliation, etc.

"Do not be deceived, God is not mocked; for whatever a man sows, this he will also reap."

Galatians 6:7

You will reap what you sow.

So what do you want to harvest in your life? Be careful what you plant. Your choice! Simple…just not easy.

IV. Freedom

I like to be free. Free to live life and experience all that God intended for us. How about you? Is your desire to be free or would you rather live in bondage? I hope you would prefer to live in freedom. What do you want to be free from? Here are a few things that I'm not fond of that have been, and in some ways continue to, plague my life. However, I've been fortunate to experience freedom from all of these and wish the same for you as well:

- Punishment of sin
- Power of sinful, destructive habits
- Inferiority and insecurity
- Fear of failure or rejection
- Anxiety or worry
- Debt
- Anger, Bitterness, Revenge

But how? How does one obtain freedom? Great question. The answer is...you guessed it...very simple but not easy. It will take effort on your part but the rewards are amazing...sound familiar? So what's the answer?

"Believe on the Lord Jesus Christ and you will be saved."   Acts 16:31

"If you abide in My Word, you are My disciples indeed, and you shall know the truth and the truth will set you free."   Jesus Christ   John 8:31-32

"I am the vine, you are the branches: He who abides in me, and I in him, bears much fruit; for without Me you can do nothing."
Jesus Christ   John 15:5

"For we are his workmanship, created in Christ Jesus unto good works, which God hath before ordained that we should walk in them."   Ephesians 2:10

"God created man in His own image, in the image of God He created him; male and female He created them. God blessed them; and God said to them, 'Be fruitful and multiply, and fill the earth, and subdue it; and rule over the fish of the sea and over the birds of the sky and over every living thing that moves on the earth.'"

Genesis 1:27-28

"That being justified by his grace, we should be made heirs according to the hope of eternal life."

Titus 3:7

"Have I not commanded you? Be strong and of good courage; do not be afraid, nor be dismayed, for the Lord your God is with you where ever you go."

Joshua 1:9

"For I am persuaded, that neither death, nor life, nor angels, nor principalities, nor powers, nor things present, nor things to come, nor height, nor depth, nor any other creature, shall be able to separate us from the love of God, which is in Christ Jesus our Lord."

Romans 8:38-39

"For He made Him who knew no sin to be sin for us, that we might become the righteousness of God in Him."
II Corinthians 5:21

"Therefore, having been justified by faith, we have peace with God through our Lord Jesus Christ, through whom also we have access by faith into this grace in which we stand, and rejoice in hope of the glory of God. And not only that, but we also glory in tribulations, knowing that tribulation produces perseverance; and perseverance, character, and character, hope. Now hope does not disappoint, because the love of God has been poured out in our hearts by the Holy Spirit who was given to us."   Romans 5:1-5

"There is therefore now no condemnation to those who are in Christ Jesus, who do not walk according to the flesh, but according to the Spirit. For the law of the Spirit of life in Christ Jesus has made me free from the law of sin and death."   Romans 8:1-2

"Stand fast therefore in the liberty by which Christ has made us free, and do not be entangled again with a yoke of bondage."   Galatians 5:1

"The thief does not come except to steal, kill, and destroy. I have come that they may have life, and that they may have it more abundantly."
                        Jesus Christ   John 10:10

Have you found the answer yet?

The answer is God.

If you know Him personally and seek His Word, His Will, His value system, and His glorification in your life, **then**

you will be free to live life to the fullest in Christ, guaranteed. It's a promise directly from God Himself, <u>it works every time and all the time</u>…it is eternal!

My "Simple but not easy" definition of **True freedom** from…

(a) Eternal punishment, i.e. the Penalty of Sin: This is the one big issue that many just don't want to deal with. But the Bible clearly says that all men fall short of God's standard due to our sin nature. Punishment for our sin as defined by the Bible is eternal separation from God. Freedom from this punishment for all eternity comes from God alone through the atonement of sin. This is possible by accepting God's grace, mercy and forgiveness through His Son, Jesus Christ. If you don't have the righteousness of Christ, then you must somehow obtain perfection, i.e. the righteousness of God, on your own.

> "God made Him who had no sin to be sin for us, so that in Him we might become the righteousness of God."
> 2 Corinthians 5:21

> "But now a righteousness from God, apart from law, has been made known, to which the Law and the Prophets testify. This righteousness from God comes through faith in Jesus Christ to all who believe."
> Romans 3:21-22

(b) Once you've secured your freedom for eternity, what about the here and now? "I still struggle with temptation and making bad choices." Really? Me too! You are not alone.

Everyone struggles with sin,

even those who have accepted Christ Jesus and have the Holy Spirit residing in your heart. We can only have victory over and freedom from the **Power of Sin** on a day to day, moment by moment basis, if we submit to and surrender control of our lives to the Holy Spirit. By living in the power of His Holy Spirit we can be free from sin on an ongoing basis. This is a choice believers in Christ make constantly. And when we submit to and allow the Holy Spirit to lead, we have victory!

> "What shall we say then? Shall we (believers in Jesus Christ) continue in sin that grace may abound? Certainly not! How shall we who died to sin live any longer in it?"   Romans 6:1-6

> "Or do you (believer in Jesus Christ) not know that your body is the temple of the Holy Spirit who is in you, whom you have from God, and you are not your own? For you were bought at a price (Christ's death on the cross); therefore, glorify God in your body and in your spirit which are God's."   1 Corinthians 6:19

(parenthesis added for context)

> "But the fruit of the Spirit is love, joy, peace, patience, kindness, goodness, faithfulness, gentleness and self control. Against such there is in no law."
>
> Galatians 5:22

A quick side note on living in the Spirit. If you are full of the Holy Spirit, then you will live by the fruits of that Spirit (Gal 5:22). Notice if you violate one of the fruits above, you violate them all. You're either full of the Spirit or you're full of yourself. And you'll know simply by looking at the "fruit" in your life! Not only is this is a great way to test your own life, it's also a great question to ask your kids from time to time to test their behavior against these fruits. Works for adults too! A great resource on living by the Spirit is Steve McVey's book, *Grace Walk*.

(c) How about **inferiority and insecurity?** Do you struggle with these at times? Have you ever wondered why you have these feelings? Do you think God wants you to feel this way? Refer back to the scriptural references at the beginning of this chapter. Do any of these verses sound like God wants you to feel this way? I challenge you to find scriptures that indicate that God wants you to have an inferiority complex or be insecure. The truth is: He loves you and sent His Son to die on a cross so you could spend eternity with Him. He wants what's best for you, for you to live life to the fullest, to bear fruit, to steward His creation, to be heirs to the Kingdom of Heaven. Inferiority and insecurity just don't fit in! At least not when we embrace the truth of how God feels about us and what He wants for us. It's simply getting in touch with, abiding in, the Truth and rejecting the falsehoods that this world and our enemy keep throwing our way. That's the "not easy" part because we have a strong adversary who is very good at turning our lives inside out!

(d) Let's try **Fear of Rejection**.

> "For I am persuaded, that neither death, nor life, nor angels, nor principalities, nor powers, nor things present, nor things to come, nor height, nor depth, nor any other creature, shall be able to separate us from the love of God, which is in Christ Jesus our Lord."
>
> Romans 8:38-39

Have you ever felt like you just didn't have the support of others; that you were all alone? Just remember the following:

> "...if God is for us, who can be against us?"
>
> Romans 8:31b

> "I can do all things through Christ who gives me strength."
> Philippians 4:13

Enough said. If you are in Christ Jesus, rejection is not possible! Or at least it shouldn't be from a BIG PICTURE perspective. See things from God's perspective. Embrace your *relational security* and *significance* in Christ! I think Tim Kimmel says it best...

"You and God make a majority <u>every time!</u>"
(Tim Kimmel, author and founder of Family Matters)

(e) Failure? I've never met anyone who likes to fail, myself included. I want to be right, just ask my wife and children! When I'm wrong, it doesn't *feel* very good, and I don't *feel* significant. But you know what? The most loving thing my family can do for me is speak the truth in love and correct me when I'm wrong! The challenge is that failure is part of life, and I believe a necessary part of life for things to work out ultimately for our own good. Failure is always a possibility, but an option I encourage you to never choose. That's right, it's completely up to you and in your control. "That's impossible" you say? Let me explain. I failed a few tests during my academic years, didn't make a particular sports team, showed up late to important events, didn't get a particular job or promotion I was hoping for....and Babe Ruth struck out how many times? I'm not all that concerned about a mistake or even a bona fide failure experience that happens once or perhaps even twice. If you are learning from your experiences, maturing and doing a better job next time, explain to me how you are in bondage to your past failures?

If you learn and always try your best, I say you can have freedom from failure.

You can turn your entire life experience into a maturing, growing process which actually requires temporary short-term failure to stimulate learning and development. You can't expect to hit a golf ball correctly and never miss-hit it again. Learning actually requires temporary periods of failure. But you should not be obsessed with and fearful of failure. Be free from that.

Embrace a failure for what it is: a temporary outcome that if learned from can make you better over time.

"Now thanks be to God who always leads us in triumph in Christ, and through us diffuses the fragrance of His knowledge in every place."

II Corinthians 2:14

"Yet in all things we are more than conquerors through Him who loved us. For I am persuaded that neither death nor life, nor angels nor principalities nor powers, nor things present or things to come, nor height nor depth, nor any other created thing, shall be able to separate us from the love of God which is in Christ Jesus our Lord."

Romans 8:37-39

"Failure is an event. Never a person"
(Zig Zigler, speaker and author)

(f) Do you get **Anxious** from time to time? About what? Is it something you have control over?   If so, then I challenge you to reject worrying about it. "But wait a minute, if it's something important, are you telling me I should ignore it?" Absolutely not. What I'm saying is eliminate w*orry* from your life and replace it with *concern*. Here's the difference.   If you are *concerned* about something, then you will do something about it! If you are *worried* about something, then you will sit there dwelling on it, probably ruin your attitude in the process, and basically do nothing about it. Worrying doesn't do you or anyone else for that matter any good.   If you can do something about it, then act. That's the "not easy" part. We all have opportunities to change our circumstances and help others. **Get up and do something about it.** If you can't, then I would argue that you're dwelling on something that is outside of your control. If this is the case, simply turn it over to God:

> "Be anxious for nothing, but in everything by prayer and supplication with thanksgiving let your requests be made known to God. And the peace of God, which surpasses all comprehension, will guard your hearts and your minds in Christ Jesus. Finally, brethren, whatever is true, whatever is honorable, whatever is right, whatever is pure, whatever is lovely, whatever is of good repute, if there is any excellence and if anything worthy of praise, dwell on these things."   Philippians 4:6-7

"Have I not commanded you? Be strong and of good courage; do not be afraid, nor be dismayed, for the Lord you God is with you where ever you go."   Joshua 1:9

Your choice. Pretty simple...just not easy.

(g) Do you like to be in **debt** and forever be paying back others what you owe? Doesn't sound very freeing to me. I personally don't like to be in debt. It's very confining and adds quite a bit of stress in life. If you think about it, once you "owe" someone, aren't you enslaved to that person or organization until you pay back what you owe? So what's the simple answer? Don't borrow! Buy things when you can afford it. The "not easy" part is *patiently* saving, practice a little *delayed gratification,* and exercise *financial discipline.* By the way, this works every time! Of course you can go into debt and get things faster, just remember that whether you go into debt or not, both are "package deals" that come with consequences. Perhaps sometimes it is necessary to borrow, but I challenge you to strongly consider whether you really *need* whatever it is you are buying and always have a plan on how you will repay your debt. If you want to be completely free, then perhaps this scripture is for you:

"For the LORD your God will bless you as He has promised you, and you will lend to many nations, but you will not borrow; and you will rule over many nations, but they will not rule over you."

Deuteronomy 15:6

■■■ı

One more point: The freedoms I have been discussing are true for believers in Christ. But while this is truth, it is not necessarily a reality in your life.

Even after we get it (become a believer in Christ), We don't always get it (act Christ-like).

To become a reality in your life…and here's the "not easy" part…you must <u>choose</u> to accept these truths, <u>abide</u> in the Lord, <u>yield </u>to the power of the Holy Spirit and <u>apply</u> them daily in your life, moment by moment.

"Take My yoke upon you and learn from Me, for I am gentle and humble in heart, and YOU WILL FIND REST FOR YOUR SOULS. For My yoke is easy and My burden is light."

Jesus Christ   Matthew 11:29-30

I pray <u>you will choose</u> to find rest for your soul and that your burden becomes light. Again, very simple…just not easy.

Chapter 5:
Prosperity in...

I. Marriage

Are you ready? Are you prepared to make the second most important decision in your life? The first most important decision is your response to the question: Who do you say Jesus is? Are you prepared to cultivate the soil, plant, water, and reap the harvest of a good marriage? In other words, <u>are you prepared to work </u>at your marriage? That's right, "work at it". Marriage, just like life in general, is not easy, it requires intentional effort for it to begin, stay healthy, grow, mature, and produce. How would you answer the following with regard to your readiness for marriage:

Do you have the proper "_____"

- "Instruction" - Do you know how?
- "Perspective" - Do you have the proper values?
- "Emotional maturity" - Do you have self control and humility?
- "Perseverance" - Are you prepared for a life-long, one-time event?
- "Commitment" - Are you prepared to put your spouse and marriage before yourself?

...for marriage? What professional athlete ever steps onto the field before first acquiring the skills necessary, practicing, and under the guidance of a trustworthy coach, engage in the game? Have you discussed those important topics with your future spouse ahead of time, topics like faith, $, sex, children, parenting, family traditions and values, career expectations, and any important personal goals?

How do you really know if you and your future spouse are compatible for a lifetime if you don't find out first?

You study reading, writing, and arithmetic for years in school. Why not do a bit of studying on marriage? Will both you and your future spouse be willing to nurture, protect, defend, strengthen, and grow your marriage?

"So what's the big deal?" you say. "My future spouse and I love each other, enjoy spending time together, are perfect for one another, and that's all that matters." I agree it is very important that you love each other, but what does it mean to "love each other"?

Gentlemen, are you ready to become a husband and show love by laying down your life, to provide for, to protect, and to **unconditionally love** your wife no matter what?

> "Husbands, love your wives, just as Christ also loved the church and gave Himself up for her, so that He might sanctify her, having cleansed her by the washing of water with the word, that He might present to Himself the church in all her glory, having no spot or wrinkle or any such thing; but that she would be holy and blameless. So husbands ought also to love their own wives as their own bodies. He who loves his own wife loves himself" Ephesians 5:25 -28

Ladies, would you like your husbands **to love you unconditionally and be willing to die for you?** I believe that is what God expects out of us husbands. And are you prepared to submit to your husband's leadership, to nurture your family, and **unconditionally respect** your husband no matter what?

"Wives, be subject to your own husbands, as to the Lord. For the husband is the head of the wife, as Christ also is the head of the church, He Himself being the Savior of the body. But as the church is subject to Christ, so also the wives ought to be to their husbands in everything." Ephesians 5:22-24

Husbands, would you like your wife **to respect you unconditionally?** And wives, would you like your husband to love you unconditionally? Sounds quite heavenly if you ask me!

Falling in love is actually rather easy. Men and women are designed to be attracted to one another physically.

It doesn't take that much investigation to find <u>attraction</u>. It does take rigorous investigation to find out <u>compatibility</u>.

Let's begin with the simple truth that...

men and women are not the same, but <u>they are equally important.</u>

The two sexes are very different and have different needs, different roles, and different challenges. This is by God's design and by His system, not mine, and each is a "package deal." To mix and match will add great complexity and difficultly to your life, your marriage, and your ability to constructively impact others.

Let's explore what I've found to be the key non-physical difference between *most* men and *most* women a bit more:

Significance vs. Relational Security.

I was first introduced this concept while taking Dr. Marlin Howe's marriage enrichment seminar, "Hope for the Family."[1] Dr. Howe made the point the these two things, significance and relational security, are basic needs for each one of us. From that point forward, I've been amazed at how many times I see these two themes rise to the surface in business seminars, TV shows and movies, and in our day to day lives. We all need some of both. However, I found that in general...

a man's primary need is for significance while a woman's primary need is for relational security.

Why do I say that? Well let's examine the evidence. What do men spend their time doing vs. women? I believe it has nothing to do with economics, cultural trends, politics, personalities or religion. And I also believe it has nothing to do with opinion, yours or mine. Men and women naturally (or by intentional design by our Creator) gravitate towards certain activities.

[1] © 1993 HOPE FOR THE FAMILY by Dr. Marlin Howe

This is simply an observation over one man's lifetime supported by actual experience, confirmed by others in my life, and revealed by Biblical Truth.

In general, you will find that...

Men focus more on goal-oriented activities while women focus more on process-oriented activities.

You can argue the point but I challenge you to look at <u>what most men and most women do with their free time and money.</u> So what distinguishes goal vs. process oriented activities? Goal-oriented activities have a clearly defined outcome or objective, while process-oriented activities are designed primarily for fellowship or socializing. This is neither good nor bad; it just is. And please understand that we all need some of both. It's just that *most* **men need more significance and** *most* **women need more relational security.** I use the term *"most"* because there are always exceptions.

What do most guys spend their time doing? From my experience: hunt, fish, challenge one another in sports, bet on card games and sporting events, work, climb mountains, snow ski, work on cars, race cars, woodwork...in other words compete, conquer, create...i.e. ***Goal-Oriented Activities***. And for most of the ladies? Again from my limited experience and observation: shop, go to the spa for new hair styles, manicures, pedicures and massages, have lunch or meet over a cup of coffee to visit, play games, craft, cook, entertain...in other words, spend time with and relate to others...i.e. **Process-Oriented Activities.**

The purpose of goal-oriented activities is the result or outcome: what are we going to accomplish and what defines winning or losing, success or failure?

Goal-oriented activities provide significance.

The purpose of process-oriented activities is building or growing the relationship: who will I be spending time with, what will we do together, and for how long?

Process-oriented activities strengthen and provide security in relationships.

Let's take this from another angle. From a very early age, what do children spend their time doing? Consider the following:

Typical activities for young boys: compete in sports, play army, wrestle, fight, build forts...all these are goal-oriented, competitive, and have a clearly defined winner or outcome; competing, conquering, defeating, winning, achieving all add significance to life.

Typical activities for young girls: play dolls, dress up, do crafts together, cook, talk, shop, beautify...these are all process-oriented with no winner or loser, it's about being together, spending time relating to one another, building strong relationships; these process-oriented activities add relational security to our lives...and yes, girls also play sports and some girls can be very competitive. There's nothing wrong with that and if you are a lady that likes competition, by all means compete!

As I said previously, the flow of time and money spent on activities is typically a good indicator of what is going on with regard to basic needs. What do men and women spend their time and money doing? Both sexes naturally gravitate towards those activities that enhance their lives the most. Otherwise, why would they do them in the first place? Please remember, everyone whether male or female, needs both, and the mixture of goal vs. process-oriented activities will vary from person to person.

What I find interesting is what the Bible has to say about men's and women's' relationships in the context of a marriage. God clearly and very distinctly instructs both the husband and the wife in dealing with the opposite sex:

> "Nevertheless, each individual among you also is to love his own wife even as himself, and the wife must see to it that she respects her husband." Ephesians 5:33

- Husbands are to **unconditionally love**. Why? Because that's what the wife needs *most*, relational security.

- Wives are to **unconditionally respect**. Why? Because that's what the husband needs *most*, significance.

Scripture is very consistent here and that's an indication to me that there's an intelligent, creation connection here:

God designed marriage, men, and women. He knows what it takes for our relationships and our marriages to work properly.

Another very important point I need to make is that both the husband and the wife are to be aligned spiritually. The Bible refers to this as being "equally yoked"...

> "Do not be bound together with unbelievers; for what partnership have righteousness and lawlessness, or what fellowship has light with darkness?"
>
> 2 Corinthians 6:14

If the husband and wife are on different pages spiritually, you can image the conflict, frustration, and complexity that result. My observation for couples in this category, i.e. those couples who are "unequally yoked", is that simplicity will be a major challenge and the not-easiness of life is much greater.

So let's take a break for a humorous departure on men understanding women. Being a man myself and living with my wife and three daughters, I can relate to what I'm about to share. One thing us men need to come to grips with is that no matter how much we study or how hard we try, <u>we will never completely understand</u> what makes a woman act, say, think, and do the things she does when she does them. The same can probably be said from a woman's perspective concerning men. Anyway, the following joke sum's up my point perfectly:

A man walking along a California beach was deep in prayer. All of sudden, he said out loud, "Lord grant me one wish."

Suddenly the sky clouded above his head and in a booming voice the Lord said, "Because you have tried to be faithful to me always, I will grant you one wish."

The man said, "Build a bridge to Hawaii, so I can drive over anytime I want to". The Lord said, "Your request is very materialistic. Think of the logistics of that kind of undertaking. The supports required to reach the bottom of the Pacific! The concrete and steel it would take! I can do it, but it is hard for me to justify your desire for worldly things. Take a little more time and think of another wish, a wish you think would honor and glorify Me.

The man thought about it for a long time. Finally he said, "Lord, help me to understand women. I want to know how they feel inside, what they are thinking when they give me the silent treatment, why they cry, what they mean when they say 'nothing,' and how I can make a woman truly happy."

After a few minutes God said.........."You want two lanes or four lanes on that bridge?"

(author unknown)

After sharing this joke with my wife and three daughters, they quickly agreed that I have a tendency to "not get" things! And one day when my wife saw the confused look on my face as I watched one of my daughters behave rather strangely, she gently instructed me to go "build a bridge." I love my wife!

So let's get back to marriage...

When two members of the opposite sex get married, what often follows? You are correct, marriage often times leads to offspring. Before you get married, please consider whether you are ready to become a parent and *steward another life*, your children's life, from adolescence to responsible adulthood?

Are you ready to raise your offspring, the future parents of your grandchildren?

Yes, that's correct. You should be thinking very long-term prior to making this decision. Will my spouse and I be able to provide a home capable of raising the next generation and the parents of the generation after? Are you considering your grandchildren in this decision?

"Well I don't want to think about that right now! I just want to experience my future spouse and enjoy the blessings of our relationship now!"

That's fine if you want to take that short-term approach. Excuse me for saying this but in my opinion that's rather selfish. I'm not trying to be insensitive here. This is a very significant step in life, and I want you to be prepared and for your marriage to be a tremendous blessing to you, your spouse, and any future offspring. This isn't short-term. Marriage is life-long, "till death do us part." What you decide today will impact the future, YOUR FUTURE. Let me repeat that:

What you decide today and set in motion will create a future family system with the likelihood of creating future children that will be influenced by that family system you and your spouse have created; children that will likely grow up to become adults and the parents of the next generation.

That's the truth. You may think your life is just your own right now and nobody else's, to be enjoyed by just you; however, combine it with a member of the opposite sex, bring children into the equation, and you have just impacted a whole new generation. **This is serious and should not be taken lightly.**

110

Becoming a spouse - and even better a parent - is a **TREMENDOUS BLESSING** if you approach it with a stewardship mentality.

There is no greater source of significance or relational security created than from a strong marriage and family system

...that unconditionally loves and respects, completes one another, and raises new generations to do the same. That is awesome and by God's perfect design!

Just realize that if you choose...yes, IT'S YOUR CHOICE, your free will, your responsibility...to ignore these realities, truths, and consequences, you will eventually have to deal with all the issues I've been talking about. And oh how I pray that you do not find out one day that you and your spouse have some compatibility issues in those important aspects of your life. If this happens, I can assure you that your life, your marriage, your extended family, your life ambitions, and the lives of future generations will not be simple. In addition to the "not easiness" of life, you will add to your already full plate: complexity, stress, relational strain, frustration, hurt, debate or worse... disagreement and division. If you're not thinking along these long-term lines before you tie the knot, then I challenge whether you are mature enough for a good, solid, long-term godly marriage.

You may be prepared to *enjoy* your spouse and the relational and physical blessings of marriage in the near-term..."for better", "in health", and "for richer", but are you prepared to *steward* your marriage long-term and fulfill the vows "for worse", "in sickness", and "for poorer"?

During a lifetime you will experience both the positives and the not-so-positives, it is inevitable. Think about that. Over an entire lifetime can you only experience the positive side of the marriage vows? No, that's not realistic; it's just not possible.

Being prepared for this life-long <u>covenant</u> is up to you.

Aside on the Marriage Covenant:
Have you ever noticed that this covenant, which means an agreement between two people **in the presence of God, is <u>unconditional?</u>** What do you promise when you get married? Don't both man and woman promise to stay together in sickness and in health, for richer or for poorer, in good times and bad, till death do us part? How will your marriage be impacted if this level of commitment is true?

Many couples don't even think about it and simply "learn as you go"; but why take the chance? This is your life, your decisions, your influence on your future spouse, your marriage, and your legacy. Let me ask this another way: what do you want your future spouse to be thinking about, the short-term or the long-term? What would your marriage be like, what kind of a start would there be to your relationship, if both of you were thinking long-term, next generation, for worse - in sickness - for poorer? Wow, talk about a solid foundation! Remember, with all things of great value such as a marriage,

you don't pay the price...you enjoy the benefits.

Marriage by God's definition is "till death due us part". It's a *life-long covenant*. Why not invest a bit of time upfront in preparation for your second most important, life-long decision?

And if you're already married and may not have fully investigated all these issues, you can begin today! You have made your choice, so it's time to avoid complaining and move forward. Will it be easy? Probably not... Life is simple, but it's never easy. It will always require effort! Don't lose sight of that. You will have to work today, tomorrow, and the next, regardless of what your past decisions have been. That's not a bad thing that you have to intentionally, and continually put effort into your marriage, it generates tremendous significance and relational security, remember? If there is no effort, then the opposite is true. You can choose to shift your thinking today to a longer-term view.

You can't change the past but you can always, repeat ALWAYS, impact the future as long as you have life.

Choose to do this if not for yourself, for your spouse and your family (if you are blessed to have offspring) and ultimately to glorify God. Don't quit, that was not intended to be an option. Marriage is life-long. What brought the two of you together can keep you together but both of you must live for the marriage and not for self, live for the offspring of your marriage and not yourself, live for the next generation and not yourself. If you put God first, your marriage second, and yourself last, you will reap blessings long-term beyond your imagination and experience greater simplicity and fullness in your life. If you don't, if you put yourself first, you may experience temporary relief, but at a cost of long-term complexity, frustration, and difficulty not only for you, but for those closest to you as well: your spouse, your children, and your children's children. Please, please, please live not for self but for God, your spouse and for your marriage, consider the bigger, long-term picture and the generations to come, that is where you will find the significance and relational security that lasts for a life time and beyond.

"So what if I've been married but it didn't work out? What if I'm no longer married? What if I've been through a divorce? Will these same principals still apply?" Absolutely! First of all, is there a chance to reconcile with your ex-spouse? That's the simple and easier solution. I would strongly consider it and get some assistance from a trustworthy, Christian source. Remember, divorce was not an intended option. I would exhaust all avenues for restoration before moving on.

> "Therefore if you are presenting your offering at the altar, and there remember that your brother has something against you, leave your offering there before the altar and go; first be reconciled to your brother, and then come and present your offering."
> Jesus Christ   Matthew 5:23-24

Did you notice that? Jesus is telling us *before* we attempt to approach God with a gift, *reconcile ourselves to others*, especially our brothers and sisters in Christ. Interestingly, a marriage should originally be **a covenant** ordained by God Himself, after all, He came up with the institution of marriage. So for two individuals who have been married before God to call it quits seems a bit inconsistent with this verse. It would make more sense to me for the two to work out their differences and live for God and their marriage and not for self. Of course, this verse is speaking to us as individuals and your spouse may reject this truth.

"If possible, so far as it depends on you, be at peace
with all men."   Romans 12:18

You can do all you can (pray, seek Godly counseling, rest
and abide in the Lord for strength and perseverance, repent
and forgive...) and it may not be enough to bring your
partner to the point of reconciliation. If it's no longer
possible to reconcile with your ex-spouse, there may be a
new opportunity in your future to start again. After all, we
worship a God of second chances. Will there still be
complexities from past decisions? Yes. Are you still
accountable to the people from the prior marriage? Yes,
especially if you have had children from a previous
marriage. Your children should be a key consideration in
how you move forward. But with a new day, you can
always begin again, and begin to promote and seek a life of
simplicity and greater ease for yourself and those closest to
you.

****

Aside on the Traditional Family...the Foundation of all
Great Societies

I feel led to add a few comments here as I am
frequently dealing with the issue of "sexual
orientation." Heterosexual relationships are
designed for procreation. They are part of God's
intelligent design. Homosexual relationships don't
make sense and to me and represent the opposite of

"intelligent design". For example, take homosexuality to extreme: imagine what would happen if everyone in the world decided to engage in that lifestyle. It wouldn't take long for there to be no more mankind! Hmm?

Many argue that some people are "born that way". I'm not convinced of this but let's explore that as a possibility. To say that is to basically say that people have been born with a natural tendency towards this or that, in this case homosexuality. Given that I am a man, I'm going to share my perspective on men; however, the general point I'm about to make applies to everyone. I can confidently say that most men are born with a natural tendency towards adultery. If you doubt this statement, just follow behaviors and money. Do men engage in pornography, "mens" clubs, extramarital affairs, premarital sex? Just look at history, culture, and the flow of money towards these activities, and it's obvious that men struggle with these sinful habits. I'm a heterosexual man who happens to find more than one woman physically attractive. I would gather that most heterosexual men would say the same thing. Does that give me or any other man the freedom to exercise our selfish desires to sleep with whatever woman interests me when ever I want? To practice adultery? Of course not! I'm a happily married man who made **a covenant** before God and in the presence of my wife, Debbie, and our loved ones to be faithful and keep myself only unto her. Does that stop temptation? Not necessarily. **Temptation should not be an invitation to sin, it should be a warning to flee!** We all have a choice. And I choose to reject the temptation and honor my wife, my marriage, and my God. And if I'm not married, if I am single, God's Word is very clear that **sex is a blessing within the boundaries of marriage**. Sex outside of marriage is adultery. That's the "simple-not easy" truth! Single men and women are still called to purity until marriage. Although I'm not ready to concede the position that homosexuals were born that way, even if it were true, that does not give anyone the right to promote or live in a manner that corrupts God's intended plan for sexuality. The Bible clearly states that adultery and homosexuality are immoral and should not be practiced.

"Do you not know that the unrighteous will not inherit the kingdom of God? Do not be deceived. Neither fornicators, nor idolaters, nor adulterers, nor homosexuals, nor sodomites, nor thieves, nor covetous, nor drunkards, nor revilers, nor extortioners will inherit the kingdom of God. And such were some of you. But you were washed, but you were sanctified, but you were justified in the name of the Lord Jesus and by the Spirit of our God. All things are lawful for me, but all things are not helpful. All things are lawful for me, but I will not be brought under the power of any. Foods for the stomach and the stomach for foods, but God will destroy both it and them. Now the body is not for sexual immorality but for the Lord and the Lord for the body. And God both raised up the Lord and will also raise us up by his power. Do you not know that your bodies are members of Christ? Shall I then take the members of Christ and make them into a harlot? Certainly not! Or do you not know that he who is joined to a harlot is one body with her? For 'the two,' He says, 'shall become one flesh.' But he who is joined to the Lord is one spirit with Him. <u>Flee from sexual immorality</u>. Every sin that a man does is outside the body, but he who commits sexual immorality sins against his own body. <u>Or do you not know that your body is the temple of the Holy Spirit who is in you</u>, whom you have from God, and you are not your own? For you were bought at a price; therefore, <u>glorify God</u> in your body and in your spirit, which are God's."

1 Corinthians 6:9-20

(underlines added for emphasis)

To <u>practice</u> sexual immorality, whether it is adultery, homosexuality, or another "alternative lifestyle" is to the detriment of those involved and does not bring honor and glory to God. I hope you can see my point. Whether you are heterosexual or have a desire towards an "alternative lifestyle", it doesn't matter. The answer is the same:

Stay within the boundaries that God, the Lord and Creator of the universe, has established.

This is not to punish us, but for our own good. And please hear me on this.

All of us struggle with sin...ALL OF US

I refer you back to my personal confession on page 24. Homosexuality is no different than adultery, greed, gossip, lying, theft, idolatry, or any other sin. WE ALL NEED HELP to overcome those selfish, sinful desires that enslave us to a life that is less than what God intended for us. Pray and seek counsel with whatever sin you are dealing with, reject the temptation to sin, and live in accordance to the will of God. Simple...just not easy.

****

So let's get back to God's design for marriage...

> "The man said, 'This is now bone of my bones, And flesh of my flesh; she shall be called woman, because she was taken out of man.' For this reason a man shall leave his father and his mother, and be joined to his wife; and they shall become one flesh."
>
> Genesis 2:23-24

A God-centered marriage forms a picture of our relationship with God. If God is at the center of your marriage and you submit to His Lordship, then as you submit yourselves to the marriage relationship, you and your spouse will live for the glory of both God and your marriage.

When 2 become 1 flesh, I like to think of the 2 becoming greater or increasing. My view is the 2 individuals become 3. "How?" Well you still have 1 man and 1 woman; two individuals with unique personalities, likes and dislikes, mannerisms, family backgrounds, etc. However, now you have added "1", a marriage bond which represents the two individuals together. From my perspective this "marriage bond" should be set beneath God who is (or should be) at the center of the marriage. As the man and woman set themselves beneath the marriage bond, they are also set beneath God. When this happens, i.e. God being at the center, then the marriage functions to glorify God, receive His provision, and completely fulfill the needs of both man and woman. It is fueled by the Holy Spirit, bears the Fruit of Spirit, glorifies the Lord, and births a family system that is fertile soil for the man and woman to realize their full potential as a couple as well as provide fertile soil for the next generation and the generation after that.

So what if God is not at the center? What then? I'd have to answer that with a question of my own. If God is not at the center, then what is? What is it that binds two people together?

- A legal document or contract in the form of a marriage certificate
- A personal commitment from two individuals
- Love for one another, feelings, emotions
- Mutual benefit, convenience

Perhaps there are more but consider this: all of the above are not permanent. A contract can be terminated. Personal commitments are only as strong as the individual that makes them and in this case it takes two individuals making and keeping the commitment. Love, feelings, emotions come and go. Mutual benefit or convenience can last for a time but eventually something will come up that requires one or both to sacrifice. My point is this: unless your marriage has God at the center, a God that never changes, is never weary, knows what's best for you and your family, is a Rock and entirely worth living for and to His glory, and is 100% for your marriage lasting a lifetime, then you're building your marriage on sand, sand that can shift or be swept away by the inevitable storms that will come in life.

Don't construct your marriage such that a bit of "bad weather" can jeopardize the future.

"Therefore whoever hears these sayings of Mine, and does them, I will liken him to a wise man who builds his house on a rock. And the rain descended, the floods came, and the winds blew and beat on that house; and it did not fall, for it was founded on the rock.

But everyone who hears these sayings of Mine, and does not do them, will like a foolish man built his house on the sand. And the rain descended, the floods came, and the winds blew and beat on that house; and it fell. And great was its fall"

Jesus Christ   Matthew 7:24-27

So what if God is at the center and you're still having problems? Well I personally guarantee you're going to have challenges from time to time in your marriage, no matter how God-centered your marriage is. Remember, there is no such thing as perpetual happiness.

All marriages require effort, sacrifice, struggle, forgiveness, and growth, which by the way can be uncomfortable!

"Consider it all joy, my brethren, when you encounter various trials, knowing that the testing of your faith produces endurance. And let endurance have its perfect result, so that you may be perfect and complete, lacking in nothing.

James 1:2-4

Replace the word "faith" with "marriage" in this Scripture. Embrace your difficulties, work through them together as a couple, and thank God that He is there with you to give you strength, wisdom, and discernment through the power of His Holy Spirit. That's the beauty of a God-centered marriage. You're not alone as man and wife. If you are equally yoked, you both have His Spirit to empower you to have a life-long, joyful, purposeful, life-giving, and **"complete, lacking in nothing" marriage**.

What kind of marriage, what kind of life are you seeking? The choice is yours. Please find some reliable books, seminars, mentors and counselors to better prepare you for this life-giving, God-glorifying relationship. I invite you to check out some resources listed in the back that have helped my marriage and been a blessing to my family.

II. Parenting

First the "Simple"...children are gifts from God, they are individual people, and they are members of your family.

Next the "Not-so-easy"...while they are adolescents and under your accountability as their parent, you should "steward" them in such a way to allow your children to maximize their potential, to multiply their "talents" (see Matthew 25:14-30), and to become responsible adults and parents of the next generation to follow.

Please consider what I have found to be true...

Marriage & parenting are the most rewarding tasks you can engage in with regard to providing <u>significance</u> and <u>relational security</u> to your life.

Let that soak in for a minute. If significance and relational security are the two primary needs we all have in common, wouldn't it make sense that we seek out a goal/process-orientated activity that provides both in major quantities?

So first the simple: children are...

(a) Gifts from God
(b) Individual People
(c) Members of your family

(a) Gifts from God...

Question: do you view children this way? What would be the opposite of a gift? Please don't gloss over this very simple concept: your view of children will shape how you parent, influence how you interact together, and ultimately have a huge impact on how your children turn out as adults. For your children's sake and for the sake of everyone who will be impacted by their lives, please begin your parenting journey from a life giving perspective: *Children are gifts from God!*

Speaking of God...our heavenly Father...our eternal parent...if you'd like to know how to raise your children, **the simple answer is to ask Him!** He's given us divine instruction in His Word, the Bible, and will impart wisdom in your life if you earnestly seek Him.

> "But if any of you lacks wisdom, let him ask of God, who gives to all generously and without reproach, and it will be given to him. But he must ask in faith without any doubting, for the one who doubts is like the surf of the sea, driven and tossed by the wind."   James 1:5-6

What I have to say is simply stories and applications from my limited, human attempt to apply what I have been taught by Him, the LORD and Creator of the universe and by those seeking Him. The truth is that...

He created me, you, every one and everything and knows what's best for each one of us.

If you don't know Him, getting to know Him is a great first step. And once you do get to know Him, He'll grow you into an awesome parent if you'll let Him.

(b) Individual People...I hope that you will agree that children are people. Why do I say that? Well too many times I see parenting styles that do not appear to align with this very simple truth. What parenting styles am I talking about? Before we go there, let me ask you a few questions. What is the key difference that distinguishes how we deal with or treat people vs. other things in our life? I would argue that it is the "relationship" that binds us together. So how do we build relationships? Simple answer: we invest our selves and our time into the lives of others, particularly our children. "Not easy" answer: it takes time, consistency, sacrifice, inconvenience, drama resolution, reconciliation, ...IT TAKES EFFORT...to grow meaningful and intimate relationships. Children are not things or objects to be dropped off, set aside, or tucked away until you as a parent have time to enjoy them or deal with them. They are people that need parents to provide, protect, nurture, discipline, train, coach, and befriend for a lifetime. They need other people to RELATE to them and provide SIGNIFICANCE and RELATIONAL SECURITY. By the way, there is another very "simple - not easy" truth that applies in all areas of your life:

You can't give away what you don't already possess.

If you truly want to raise children in such a way as to maximize their potential, **you must have and be willing to provide significance and relational security**; these are basic needs that can only come from meaningful, loving, trustworthy relationships with others. So how do you get this ability? Great question! I hope you've got the answer but if not, let me help you. Who would know how to impart relational security and significance in your life? Who would know exactly what you and I need and when? Could it be Who created us in the first place? Again, this will sound redundant but the simple truth is it all begins with the Lord God.

God has ALL the answers, ALL the power, ALL the proper motives. If you abide in Him, you will be free to live for His glory and become the person, the spouse, the parent He intended you to be.

(c) Family members: quick point here...I know we all like to say "these are my children." My challenge is when you and I say this to remember they are individuals not to be possessed but rather, welcome members of your family. Yes Lauren, Heather, and Amanda are "my children", but they are really so much more. I challenge both you and I as parents to have a broader perspective, and think of our children as ultimately the Lord's, that our children have been given to us by God for a time to parent, and that one day they will move on into a life that He has planned for them.

Chapter 6:

Practical Parenting Applications

"Dad, when we have kids, we're going to send them to you and mom so you can discipline them."

Interestingly, it has taken quite of bit of time and effort to get to the original request made by our daughters at the dinner table about one year ago, and that is to provide some practical advice in raising children. So for the next several pages, I'd like to share some "not-so-easy" **perspectives** and **applications** that benefited our family as we raised our three daughters to adulthood.

I. Survival is an Option:

> "My son, do not forget my teaching, But let your heart keep my commandments; for length of days and years of life and peace they will add to you."
>
> Proverbs 3:1-2

> "He who curses his father or his mother, his lamp will go out in time of darkness."   Proverbs 20:20

> "Honor your father and your mother, that your days may be prolonged in the land which the LORD your God gives you."
>
> Exodus 20:12

> "Children, obey your parents in the Lord, for this is right. HONOR YOUR FATHER AND MOTHER (which is the first commandment with a promise), SO THAT IT MAY BE WELL WITH YOU, AND THAT YOU MAY LIVE LONG ON THE EARTH."
>
> Ephesians 6:1-3

Simple: survival is not guaranteed; it is an option.

Not easy: Making the right, informed choice time and time again.

My point is that we all make choices. But will those choices be *informed* choices? Maybe, maybe not. What determines whether a choice is *informed* or not? Some choices will put us in harms way; other choices will tend to put us out of harms way. The more we put ourselves in harm's way, the more likely we will be hurt. We might be lucky and get away with unwise choices for a time but why take the chance? I reminded my children frequently that my survival and theirs is optional based upon the choices each one of us make, choices that influence our own lives and the lives of those closest to us. You can heed good advice or you can ignore it. The truth is I can try my best to protect my family and teach and train my children how to protect themselves. However, if they choose not to "look both ways" before crossing the street and I happen to not be there at that moment, then the consequences may be severe. Survival is an option!

II. Natural consequences:

Ever touched a pot of boiling water? Human skin, when it comes in contact with temperatures high enough to boil water, burns and it hurts like...well, a lot! It doesn't take too many times for someone to learn that touching a hot stove or putting your skin in contact with boiling water is not a good idea. You can choose to do so, but the natural consequence will always be the same. Here are some other examples of harmful natural consequences:

- Don't turn in your homework, you'll receive lower grades and you might even fail the class.
- Be mean or inconsiderate to others, you are likely to have fewer friends.
- Act irresponsibly; it will be difficult for others to trust you.

- Don't exercise and eat right, your body will deteriorate and get out of shape.
- Don't show up for work, your job performance will suffer and eventually your employer may have to let you go.

Hopefully you get the idea and to be fair, there are natural consequences that can be very positive, i.e. the opposite of the above examples can be a reality. Life has natural consequences. Whether they are good or bad is a matter of perspective. The undeniable truth is that there are natural consequences!

III. Discipline and Training

Simple: if you do not teach your children while they are in your home, if you don't discipline them to recognize healthy boundaries and outside authority, train them to be responsible and diligent, considerate of others, trustworthy, respectful...THEN...

Not Easy:...when your children leave your home and go out into the world; **the world will do the discipline and training for you.** And, you the parent (along with the rest of the world) will be dealing with a self-centered, overgrown child that might expect you to take care of their needs, wants, and life problems. Wow, that doesn't sound simple or easy at all!

Think about that. What will the world's training and discipline look like? If your child is irresponsible, how will the world teach your child to become responsible? If you child is inconsiderate and selfish, how will the world teach your child to put the needs of others first? Untrustworthy? Disrespectful? I can guarantee that if a child has not learned these character traits before they leave home, then they will face a world that typically has less patience, mercy, and grace than in their own home, not to mention a heavy dose of selfishness. And think about your adult-aged child from the world's perspective. Won't the world be expecting a well trained, respectful, responsible adult? I certainly do. If you love your children and want what's best for them long-term, please accept the simple approach and give them these gifts by way of your parenting. If you don't, the "not easiness" of life will become even more complex for <u>both you and your unprepared children</u> as they face the world.

My <u>simple</u> yet strong suggestion is that you, the parent, teach your children the basics - on respect, submission to authority, healthy boundaries in relationships, being considerate of others, and responsibility - by putting forth the <u>not easy</u> effort to love, constructively discipline, train, and coach your children as they mature and learn how to live beyond themselves and live for God and others.

IV. Next generation

BEFORE you become a parent...I suggest you begin to think long-term. If you are already a parent, then the time is now for you to think long-term! Physical, relational, spiritual survival...none are a guarantee in life and all take effort. So who is going to be responsible for these things if not today, then tomorrow? Your children might have children of their own someday. When are your kids going to learn and mature so they are prepared to teach them to their children, your grandchildren? You do love your grandchildren, don't you? **Well what kind of parents are you going to give them?** Let me repeat that...

What kind of parents are you going to give to your grandchildren?

If you are a parent right now, you are raising the parents of your future grandchildren...sounds a bit intimidating if you ask me, <u>and I think it should.</u> Parenthood should not be taken lightly. It has huge impacts on the lives of so many people.

Don't you think it would be wise to raise your children in such a way so they reach their full potential physically, relationally, and spiritually?

I'd have to say that many parents focus on the fun side of the job description and tend to forego their responsibility to raise an infant to responsible adulthood. Please don't misunderstand what I am saying. <u>Of course we should enjoy our children and have fun along the way.</u>

Fun or enjoyment in parenting will naturally occur given a healthy perspective discussed earlier.

Having fun with children does require effort; however, compared to the discipline, training, coaching aspects of parenting, the "having fun" part is relatively simple, easy and it just happens!

"But how do I discipline, train, and coach my children?" I am not an expert parent other than I have been there and continue "to parent" my three daughters. For example, to this day I still remind them occasionally to "use their manners." You would think after 18 to 21 years of instruction they would be good to go. No, they still need a gentle reminder every now and then, particularly when they are speaking to mom and dad!

So where should you go to get some good parenting advise? Step 1 should always be to pray, preferably with your spouse. Pray for guidance, wisdom, discernment, and lots of patience. Pray for your children to learn, grown, and mature. Pray for both you and your children to do the following:

> "But examine everything carefully; hold fast to that which is good..."   1Thessolonians 5:21

Step 2 is to seek out good advice. There are lots of good books out there for getting parenting instruction. But before going there I must repeat myself. You can get all the "head" knowledge you want, and I believe still miss the mark. Knowledge is good, but…

without the power of God's Holy Spirit residing in your <u>heart</u>…

you will not have the proper motives and endurance necessary to preserve, to parent selflessly, and to God's glory. If you already have His Holy Spirit, then begin with the Bible, God's Word, the Ultimate Authority. In addition, there are many excellent resources available that provide experiential and life applications of Biblical Truth. If you are fortunate to have some good mentors in your life, wonderful, learn from them. Accountability with other parents that you respect is a great way to reinforce your parenting. However, as you seek out Godly instruction in this area, *test everything against God's Word*. After all, you are engaging in an activity and a responsibility that will impact many people including a whole new generation.

V. Relationship Priorities

According to *Growing Kids God's Way* by Gary and Anne Marie Ezzo…

"There are two related evils that threaten successful parenting and lead to the demise of the family. The first is downplaying the significance of the husband-wife relationship in the parenting process, and the second is falling into the entrapment of child-centered parenting. To avoid these threats, parents must learn early on that God preprogrammed all factors for success into His divine plan. As with all matters discussed in Scripture, if you violate the principles, you forfeit the blessings. When you embrace His commandments, the blessings of joy and fulfillment will be yours."[1]

Chapter: Right Beginnings; p. 57
Gary and Marie Ezzo, 1998, "Growing Kids God's Way" (4th Edition), Micah 6:8 Simi Valley, California

Two points that I'd like to emphasize here:

(1) The marriage between Mom and Dad must come first. It is the foundation of the family. It is the most important gift you can give to your children. And if you do make the marriage relationship primary, I believe that will take care of "child-centered" parenting.

(2) It's a choice. You can choose to prioritize the marriage or not. You can choose to parent by centering your attention on your child. Just remember, choices have consequences. Please examine the "fruit" from child-centered parenting vs. the "fruit" from marriage-centered parenting and please make an informed choice.

By the way, Debbie and I found *Growing Kids God's Way* very beneficial in equipping us with Biblically based parenting perspectives and approaches to discipline, train, coach, and ultimately develop friendships with our three girls. I highly recommend *Growing Kids God's Way* or similar Biblically-based parenting materials to help you in your marriage and parenting as well.

My experience has shown that a healthy family system has God in the center with the wife and husband as the core. As children are added, they become welcome members of an already established family and are attached to the core.

Children should not become the center of the family.

Very simple...God...mom/dad...then children. If you take God out of the driver's seat, you'll be relying on the abilities of two finite people, mom and dad, each with their own weaknesses and vulnerabilities. If you take mom or dad out, then you're down to relying on only one. If you take out both mom and dad out of the driver's seat, then you're relying on the children to guide your family.

Do you really want your children running the show?

Which scenario do you want? My "simple" recommendation: <u>intentional "not-easy" effort by two mature adults</u> to maintain a healthy priority in the dynamic nature of a family system.

VI. Clear communication...

"Plan-Options-Emotion"

- What's the plan?
- What are my options?
- And please tell me in a gentle, peaceful, respectful tone of voice

Do you like to be informed, to know what's going on and why? Do you like to have options and a choice? Do you like others to talk to you in a respectful, peaceful, non-threatening tone? Of course you do. Now sometimes special circumstances, such as emergencies or dealing with hysterical or violent behaviors arise that require a different approach, but these are the exception. Most often we can **choose to involve** the other person whether they are a friend, spouse, or in this case your child. And yes, when it comes to your children, age matters and you obviously don't communicate the same information to an infant as you would with a young adult. So here are a couple of things to consider...

Tell me and I might forget.
Show me and I might remember.
Involve me and I'll understand.
(Chinese Proverb)

139

Most of us prefer to be "involved" in the lives of others. You can't involve everyone. However, I challenge you to consider whether or not you are involving the right people into your life, particularly at home. If you like to be involved, then perhaps you should involve others. The simple truth is...

> "Treat others the same way you want them to treat you. "   Jesus Christ   Luke 6:31

The tough part is consistently applying this very simple yet very powerful truth in your life. Give your children the gift of reasonable choices and let them practice making decisions on their own and realizing the consequences of their decisions. Will they always make the right choice? Of course not. Allow the consequences either natural or those imposed by you the parent to take effect. Remember, these consequences can be favorable or unfavorable depending on the choices made. One final thought on communication: the sooner you can communicate with your children in a mature manner, do it. You'll model good communication, encourage them to think and make decisions for themselves, and in general help them mature as a person.

VII. Consistency

Setting precedence is a wonderful thing if you're setting the right ones and devastating if you're setting the wrong ones. If your decisions as the adult leader in the family stand, i.e.

what you say goes all the time, then once you've had your say, the decision is made and you can move on to other challenges. However, if what you say sometimes goes or doesn't at all, then you've just begun a very complex, confusing, and often times heated debate at best and an argument at worst. Your indecisiveness, your indecisions, your lack of following through will create difficulty getting past seemingly trivial tasks, and frustration will mount. Let your "yes" be yes, and your "no' be no.

> "But let your 'Yes' be 'Yes' and your 'No' be 'No,'
> for whatever is more than these is from the evil one."
>   Jesus Christ   Matthew 5:37

Simple…just not easy!

VIII. Alignment between parents

I've found alignment between parents is critical in raising your children. Children will discover where the differences lie between mom and dad and gravitate towards the parent that fulfills their selfish desires. With a very young child, this typically is not good as the child is immature and rarely knows what's best in the long run. If there are significant differences in parenting styles, expectations, standards, etc., you'll find you are not just raising a child, you'll be adding conflict with your spouse as well. It's challenging enough to pour yourself into your child without having to deal with adult conflicts at the same time.

Discuss ahead of time and agree with your spouse as to your expectations of your children.

Some issues to think about include boundaries, discipline, privileges vs. rights, wants vs. needs, manners, chores, and other home responsibilities. Keep it simple, consistent and aligned then work at it (not easy) with your spouse as a team!

IX. Effective and loving discipline

Clear boundaries must be communicated ahead of any discipline. Disobedience cannot occur until someone has clearly established and communicated a boundary. And please don't have *too many* boundaries. In other words,

don't exasperate your children by boxing them into a very narrow, confining, burdensome list of rules and regulations.

"Children, obey your parents in the Lord, for this is right. 'Honor your father and mother,' which is the first commandment with promise: 'that it may go well with you and you may live long on the earth.' And fathers, do not provoke your children to wrath, but bring them up in the training and admonition of the Lord."

Ephesians 6:1-4

Keep it simple. Decide what is most important and establish "no kidding" boundaries that you will hold your children accountable to consistently…as in EVERY TIME! As for the rest, work along side your child to establish good practices that will enrich their life and yours as well.

"So what happens if my child disobeys me as the parent?" Great question. Let's first go to the Bible and see what it has to say about instruction and discipline?

"My son, do not reject the discipline of the LORD or loathe His reproof, for whom the LORD loves He reproves, even as a father corrects the son in whom he delights. How blessed is the man who finds wisdom and the man who gains understanding."
Proverbs 3:11-13

"Whoever loves discipline loves knowledge, but he who hates reproof is stupid."
Proverbs 12:1

"A wise son accepts his father's discipline, but a scoffer does not listen to rebuke." Proverbs 13:1

"Poverty and shame will come to him who neglects discipline, but he who regards reproof will be honored."
Proverbs 13:18

"He who withholds his rod hates his son, but he who loves him disciplines him diligently." Proverbs 13:24

"A fool rejects his father's discipline, but he who regards reproof is sensible." Proverbs 15:5

"He who neglects discipline despises himself, but he who listens to reproof acquires understanding."

Proverbs 15:32

"Foolishness is bound up in the heart of a child; the rod of discipline will remove it far from him."

Proverbs 22:15

"Apply your heart to discipline and your ears to words of knowledge. Do not hold back discipline from the child, although you strike him with the rod, he will not die. You shall strike him with the rod and rescue his soul from Sheol."   Proverbs 23:12 - 14

"Discipline your son while there is hope, and do not desire his death."   Proverbs 19:18

"Listen to counsel and accept discipline, that you may be wise the rest of your days."   Proverbs 19:20

"Cease listening, my son, to discipline, and you will stray from the words of knowledge."   Proverbs 19:27

"Foolishness is bound up in the heart of a child; the rod of discipline will remove it far from him."

Proverbs 22:15

"Do not hold back discipline from the child, although you strike him with the rod, he will not die."

Proverbs 23:13

"Fathers, do not provoke your children to anger, but bring them up in the discipline and instruction of the Lord." Ephesians 6:4

"All Scripture is inspired by God and profitable for teaching, for reproof, for correction, for training in righteousness; so that the man of God may be adequate, equipped for every good work." 2 Timothy 3:16-17

"It is for discipline that you endure; God deals with you as with sons; for what son is there whom his father does not discipline? But if you are without discipline, of which all have become partakers, then you are illegitimate children and not sons. Furthermore, we had earthly fathers to discipline us, and we respected them; shall we not much rather be subject to the Father of spirits, and live? For they disciplined us for a short time as seemed best to them, but He disciplines us for our good, so that we may share His holiness. All discipline for the moment seems not to be joyful, but sorrowful; yet to those who have been trained by it, afterwards it yields the peaceful fruit of righteousness." Hebrews 12:7-11

My conclusion from reading these Scriptures is that...

discipline is necessary and good for us,

and without it, we are going down a path that will result in unfavorable outcomes. Do you know of any undisciplined people in your life? How would you describe their life?

Do they have their act together? Do they build, construct, or enhance the lives of others? Do they build, construct, or enhance your life? What about disciplined people in your life? How are they different compared with undisciplined people?

Parents, you must "discipline" your children; however, you should refrain from "punishing" them.

Why do I say that? What's the difference? Take a look at the following chart:

Punishment	Discipline
Self serving (by the person in charge)	Others serving; Sacrificial
Convenient, get it over quickly	Inconvenient, requires investing time in others
Near-term focus	Long-term focus
Strains relationships	Grows relationships
Temporarily removes bad behavior	Permanently removes bad behavior
Not healthy long-term, hinders growth	Necessary for maturing process long-term

So please discipline your children...**all the time**. However, punishment should be avoided unless absolutely necessary.

There may be times when you have an emergency and a quick response, i.e. punishment, is needed. However, as your child matures, interactions involving correction should look more and more like "discipline" and less and less like "punishment". Interact with your child for their benefit AND yours!

So getting back to the original question of what to do if your child disobeys you. My simple answer:

You must calmly administer the consequence you have already communicated to your child ahead of time.

If you've established that saying "no" to a direct command means a "time out", a loss of a certain privilege, or a spanking, then it's time for the established consequence to take affect. I would also suggest that before administering any discipline, you <u>calmly discuss</u> the situation with your child. If you can't calmly discuss it, you the parent should take a "time out" and let your emotions settle down. You should

NEVER DISCIPLINE IN ANGER.

It gives the appearance of you, the parent, being out of control, creates a very scary, threatening home environment, and becomes "punishment" instead of "discipline". Mom or Dad, you calm down first, pray about it, then as calmly as possible let your child explain what they did wrong. If your child is unable to do this, you may need to assist explaining what they did wrong and why they are being disciplined. This is no time for debate. It's time for everyone to face and <u>deal with the truth.</u> Make sure you have your facts straight. Early on your child is not likely going to embrace discipline, but they need to learn to be honest about their actions relative to clearly established boundaries set by you, the parent. They should be the ones explaining to you how their behavior meets or does not meet the boundaries you establish. If they aren't being honest, then you've got another problem to deal with. Once they've admitted their disobedience, you should give them the opportunity to apologize and better yet, repent. To repent is to turn away from a sinful behavior and pursue a different path. If they are sincere, then willingly accept their apology and restore the relationship. Note, this does not excuse the consequence that you set out from the beginning. The apology restores the relationship between you the parent and your child. The discipline or consequence should still be administered. "But wait a minute, that doesn't sound very gracious or merciful?" What you need to remember is just like with the hot stove, I can forgive my child (restore relationship) for touching it, but I can't take the burn away (consequence). If you don't allow the consequence to take affect, you are diminishing your authority and teaching the child that they can do whatever they want and simply say "sorry" to avoid any consequence.

They must be held accountable to the boundary and the consequence of that boundary, or the boundary simply becomes a guideline or suggestion.

Children need **healthy boundaries with consequences** to survive and mature. Obviously this will be age appropriate and you'll need to balance your approach, expectations, and consequences relative to their age and maturity level.

So what about spanking?
Ok, let's discuss this. Debbie and I used spanking as part of our children's discipline when they were very young. Why? We based this on instruction we received from the Bible and with programs such as *Growing Kids God's Way.* We also found that when administered in a loving, disciplined, non-threatening manner our children learned quickly, and

MORE IMPORTANTLY our relationship with our children grew more intimate.

Please don't miss out on this very important point. When you as a parent discipline properly, whether it be through a loving "spanking" or some other consequence,

you deepen the relationship with your child

and your child becomes more equipped to "self-discipline" themselves. Each discipline situation you as a parent will face is unique and there is no "one size fits all" solution.

I encourage you (and your spouse depending on your individual circumstance) to seek out instruction, study, and agree on how best to discipline your family. I've included several resources in the back that have been a blessing to our family along the way.

X. The Pacifier Principal...everyone has one!

Why do you give a baby or infant a pacifier? Well to pacify them of course! It gives them something to do with their mouth besides moan, cry or scream, right? For all three of my children, their pacifier was their most prize possession. As such, it was my opinion that...

their pacifier was a privilege.

They earned this privilege by behaving in a reasonable, generally obedient fashion. What did Debbie and I do when our children acted up or misbehaved? We took their pacifier away. Sounds counter intuitive; however, I challenge you to consider the following definition of a "pacifier":

Some thing in your life that greatly enhances it
but is not necessary for survival. It is a privilege
that you have because your behavior is overall
constructive and beneficial to those around you.

If you get your "pacifier" when you act up, then what does the pacifier become? It becomes an encouragement to "act up"! So if I misbehave, I get what I want the most? Really? That doesn't make much sense to me. Yet I see this happen all the time with parents rewarding their children for misbehaving! In our home, I was amazing to see how quickly our children would change over to more favorable behavior upon having their "pacifier" pulled! While most parents were giving their children pacifiers to *temporarily pacify*, Debbie and I were pulling "pacifiers" to discourage poor behavior, and giving them "pacifiers" as a reward for good behavior for the long-term to *more permanently pacify*. OK, now don't get too technical when it comes to a real pacifier. There was a time in the development of our children that a real pacifier assisted them as their teeth developed. I'm not talking about that. I'm talking about *privileges*. Some other examples include:

- Extended bedtimes
- Certain toys, video games, or TV shows
- Extracurricular activities
- Special foods or treats
- Cars and driving privileges (for children with drivers licenses, of course)
- Freedom to manage discretionary time

We all have a "pacifier". For me in my adult years it's free time to fish or play golf. I don't need these activities, however, I enjoy them and they help me to relax. Your job as a parent is to discern your children's "pacifier" or privilege and make sure that privileges are earned consequences from the desired behavior.

XI. Having a long-term perspective

What is the best gift you can give your children? The basics of food, shelter, and clothing? Protection and security? Your love and affection? Knowledge and wisdom? What about a spiritual foundation? All of these are good answers. One way to simply sum this up for me is as follows:

Raise your children to be awesome parents for your grandchildren!

Do everything as a parent in the context of a long-term goal of raising responsible, emotionally and spiritually mature adults that can handle the awesome responsibility of raising your grandchildren! You won't be around forever. Give your children and your grandchildren the gift of "ableness"...able to take care of themselves, have strong and meaningful relationships, and the maturity to take on and handle the responsibilities of life with excellence. If you're in a difficult situation or phase in your child's development, ask yourself what are the potential benefits of this short-term discomfort? Will a time of short-term discomfort eventually lead to maturing my child? Make the most of your opportunities to "teach them to fish for a lifetime" rather than simply "give them a fish for a day". <u>And above all, introduce them to the Lord Jesus Christ,</u> for He will make them into the Godly men and women that He designed them to be!

XII. "Teenager" is not an option

My wife and I decided never to have any teenagers. "Wait a minute, don't you have 3 children?" Well, yes we do; we just never had any "teenagers". "Well didn't they live through ages 13-19?" Of course they did. Let me explain.

The simple answer is that we never gave our children that option. As far as we were concerned, they had and still have only 4 options and really only 3 choices on how to describe their behavior. The following chart summaries these choices:

	Option	Approximate Age	Decisions Made	Responsibility Level
1	Infant	0 - 4	None	None
2	Child	4 - 10	Very Few	Little
3	Young Adult	10 - 16	Some	Some
4	Adult	16 +	All	A Lot

The age ranges above will vary depending on the child, the pace at which they mature, and there will be overlap. We view the infant stage as a given starting point for all of us and not something anyone chooses to do. We also don't know of anyone who has chosen to go back to the infant stage and all that goes along with it. So the practical choices for my children were: child, young adult, or adult, and we told them that we, the parents, would treat them according to how they behaved. Obviously most young children lack the social or mental skills to act like an adult, at least not early in life. However, as they mature, they gradually began to grow and develop the capabilities to begin acting in a more advanced stage. So how did we determine whether our children were behaving in a particular category? Well this is where you come in as a parent. How you define your expectations of your children will significantly influence their behavior. I would think seriously about that and make sure you are aligned with your spouse. Another way of saying this is as follows:

If you see a behavior, it's encouraged.

This goes for both good and bad behavior and can be generally applied not only in parenting but at work, sports, politics, you name it. Anywhere people interact this principle will apply, but for now, let's just stick with parenting. For example, let's say your 4 year old child throws a tantrum because they aren't getting something they want (notice I did not say "need"). Your child may want attention, a toy, something to eat, to participate in an activity, etc. What will your response be? If you decide to give the child what they want in order to appease them and bring peace temporarily back into the world, you have just encouraged your child to throw tantrums whenever they "want" something. In affect you have taken the easy way out and in turn greatly complicated life for both you and your child in the long run. So what is your other option? Well, it is the "simple - not easy" option! If you see an undesirable, harmful behavior in your child, you should "discourage" it through proper discipline. If you don't, then by default you are encouraging it. And when it comes to parenting, your child will misbehave, it's part of growing up. The real question is how are you, mom or dad, going to decide to parent?

So what about the positive side of the scale? You should constantly look for opportunities to praise your child for the right behaviors. Positive reinforcement is very powerful and is much more enjoyable than the negative. Let's say your child politely asks you for something or permission to do a certain activity. You should shower them with praise and if appropriate, allow them their request. Remember, you're the adult and you need to exercise your authority to ultimately determine what is best for your family at that particular time. However, I must emphasize that if you are unbalanced, if you only rely on the positive and avoid the negative side of discipline (or visa versa), you are asking for complexity and extra "not easiness" in the long run. A balanced approach will benefit both parent and child now and in the long run.

So how does all this relate to "teenagers"? Well, I define the "teenage" package as someone who wants the benefits of being a young adult - freedoms, decision making, etc. - while at the same time having the responsibility level of a child - little to none. That's not going to happen in our house! Your choices are "package deals". If you act like a child, then we as the parents are going to make most of your decisions for you and your freedoms will be limited. If, however, you act like a young adult or even better an adult, then we will allow you over time to make more and more of your own decisions, have greater <u>freedoms, privileges, and responsibilities</u> as you mature. The key is attitude and a recognition that freedom and responsibility go hand in hand. Is it wrong to act like a child? Certainly not if you have a child that is at that stage in their life! Let them be a kid, just don't give them freedoms and options that aren't suited for their maturity level. Teach them and gradually increase their freedoms and responsibilities as they learn to handle them properly in a healthy balance.

So will your children "act" like "teenagers"? They probably will from time to time. The key is to respond as the parent in an appropriate manner so as to encourage the right behaviors. If you don't like how your kids are behaving, I challenge you to evaluate how you are responding to their behaviors - how you are parenting - and whether or not this is contributing to "see a behavior, it's encouraged"? Define for your family the behaviors a "lady" or "gentlemen" would exhibit. Model these behaviors for your children and reinforce those behaviors as you discourage those unwanted behaviors.

XIII. The Defining Moment

There comes a time in the parent-child relationship when the issue of authority is seriously tested for the first time. I call this the "Defining Moment" when you as the parent need to inform your child that you are the "parent", meaning you are in authority over them while they are still a "child". It is very important that you clearly establish this very simple concept early in your parent-child relationship. This often occurs once the child is able to move about and begin to make decisions on their own. Some very clear and unforgettable memories from our past:

Lauren, our oldest, had open heart surgery when she was 2 days old. As such, we had to be very careful of her health, and she had special medications that as far as Debbie and I were concerned, she did not have the option of taking - remember, survival is an option! This medicine was pink, tasted like bubble gum and came in a liquid form which we gave to her in a test tube looking device with a spoon shaped opening. One day when she was about 2 ½ years old, we took a break from playing in the living room, and I handed her the medicine. Lauren looked me straight in the eye, sweetly said "no", and turned away to resume play. The day had finally arrived when our first child challenged our authority as parents. My response? I gently picked up Lauren and calmly explained to her that the medicine was necessary and that she had to take it. "No". I carried her back to the master bedroom and sat down on the bed, holding Lauren in one arm and the medicine in the other. I *calmly* explained that we (she and I) were going to sit on the bed until she decided to willingly take the medicine from my hand and swallow it. We were both essentially in "time out". "No Daddy" was her response with a look away and an attempt to escape my grasp. I carefully held her in one arm and the medicine in the other and repeated that her choices were to stay on the bed in my arms or willingly take her medicine, and that time permitting we would play afterwards (Plan-Options-Emotion). "No." Needless to say I was not having much fun but knew that this was the moment of truth. She needed to understand that my "yes" was a "yes" regardless of whether she understood or not. So what happened? She squirmed and moaned and tried to escape, but I did not yield. After an hour and a half, yes…90 minutes of "time out" testing of wills…she finally reached out grabbed her medicine and took it. I praised her for making the right decision and we immediately went and resumed playing. A couple of points to make:

- I joined Lauren in her "discipline" of time out. I, the parent, was willing to assume the same consequence for her disobedience; I sacrificed my freedom as well. *Now Who else did that?*
- I did not threaten or harm Lauren. She was never in danger, she simply had a privilege pulled, that being freedom to play, and a choice to make.
- I did not physically force her to take her medicine. Rather, I waited patiently until she made the right decision to exercise her free will, obey, and take it herself. It was her choice to remain in bondage or be "free.
- I did not punish her afterwards *for taking an hour and a half* out of my day to make her final decision. Instead, I encouraged her to continue making good decisions.
- I had the honor of spending 90 minutes of quality time with my daughter!

So what was the result? Well, from then on, Lauren understood that Dad and Mom were in charge, that they were willing to go the distance. That her parents were willing to sacrifice whatever was needed, and over a period of time she came to understand that the boundaries Debbie and I set were meant for her benefit. Did she ever challenge our authority again and did we have to reinforce this concept? Of course. But this day *began* Lauren's understanding that she was the child and Debbie and I were the parents. Yes this cost Lauren and I an hour and a half on the bed, but we gained a beginning of a life-long understanding of parental authority. Did we pay the price or enjoy a lifetime of benefit? I'll let you be the judge.

2010 Father's Day note from Lauren...with her permission, of course!

Happy Father's Day!
My Lord, my God, You have blessed me with a father so on fire for You. He is one of the greatest blessings in my life and for that I am truly grateful. His is my parent, teammate, friend, guide, advisor, helper, provider, and protector. He is the earthly man right now that truly rocks my world. He pushes me and encourages me like no one else. He is transparent in grace and mercy with a perspective of the world like no one else. He is the independent party that everyone wants. He understands how the world works from a Biblical view. I am so proud

to say that he is "my" dad! I am so honored to be counted among his daughters. I love him so much. I picture him a lot as the earthly vision of You. You shine right through him and all can see that. I know he does not come close in comparison to You, but it is nice to call him mine. Happy Father's Day to the ultimate Father and Happy Father's Day to Dad too! You both I love so much and pray that this day is special for both of you. Amen-

Love, Lauren

Heather, our second daughter, loved to read. We would read book after book, night after night. One day when she was also about 2 ½ years old, Debbie and I decided that it was time for her to "help" us pick up the dozen or so books left strung about the living room each night and place them back in the basket where the books were kept. Her older sister had helped pick up but for some reason Heather had not yet grasped this concept. "Heather, let's help pick up the books tonight". "No" was her response. Just to be clear, we repeated ourselves as this time it involved both Debbie and I. "No" with a very deliberate look into both of our disbelieving faces! So now it was time for our sweet little Heather to challenge our authority as parents? Heather had been so compliant up to this point and had never even hinted at disobedience. We calmly explained to Heather that she was a big girl now and needed to help the family (i.e. Mom, Dad, and Lauren…Amanda was not old enough yet) pick up after reading time. "No". It was unfortunately or fortunately time to define roles. We calmly explained to Heather that it was her decision: her choices were to help clean up or be disciplined in the form of a spanking. "No." We took her into the bedroom, calmly explained what she had done and why she was being disciplined, and gave her a firm but hardly painful spank on her bottom. After some tears, based more on the uncomfortableness of being disciplined and gentle hugs and rocking, she calmed down, and we explained again why she had been disciplined and why we were going to return to the living room to help pick up the books. Upon returning the living room..."No" with a direct stare into the eyes of both Debbie and I. "Really" Ugh! Here we go again. We repeated the same lengthy explanation of options and discipline sequence again. The spanking was hardly more than a firm tap but the calm, deliberate administration was very uncomfortable and very clear as to who was in charge. Same outcome, same tears, same parental anguish, same comfort, same return trip to the living room, but this time, we handed Heather the books and placed her by the basket. All she had to do was let the books go! Our sweet, compliant, never-a-problem-child Heather had a golden opportunity to simply let go...thinking to myself - please just let the books drop from your hands..."No". Are you kidding me! What must we parents do to get this concept through? I breathed deep, and calmly went back to the bedroom where we repeated the explanation of why we were dealing with this issue. Heather acknowledged why we were in this repetitious cycle...same firm, uncomfortable, calm, non-threatening spank, same tears, same comfort, same return to the living room...but this time she ran to pick up a book and place it in the basket....Hurray! We complimented her, hugged, kissed, and encouraged her...another book into the basket. Collectively, the books were returned in no time and the hugs and kisses were plentiful. So what was different? I'm not entirely sure. Did we do everything right? Would I have continued repeating the process? Again, I'm not quite sure. Each child is different, and Debbie and I are no experts. This is simply Debbie's and my experience with our daughter. And as with Lauren, we were challenged again but each time, a reinforcing of the roles not only clarified the concept of obedience, but deepened our relationship with each other. A few summary points:

So what was the result? Well from then on, Heather understood that Dad and Mom were in charge, that they were willing stick with decisions and boundaries, that they were willing to sacrifice whatever was needed, and overtime she came to understand that the boundaries Debbie and I set were meant for her benefit. Did she ever challenge our authority again and did we have to reinforce this concept? Of course. But this day *began* Heather's understanding that she was the child and Debbie and I were the parents. Yes this cost Heather, Debbie and I a very uncomfortable time of discipline, but we gained a beginning for a life-long understanding of parental authority. Did we pay the price or enjoy a lifetime of benefit? I'll let you be the judge.

2010 Fathers Day Note from Heather...with her permission, of course!

Dear Daddy, Happy Father's Day!
You are a tremendous blessing in my life. I hope you have a very special day because you definitely deserve it. Where do I even start, Dad? The Lord has placed you in my life to be a model of His grace, patience, discipline, and unconditional love. Thank you for loving me enough to discipline me and for coaching me through conflict with friends and family. The Lord's wisdom always pours out of you during our discussions whether we're running, driving, walking or just sitting around and hanging out. Your gray hair definitely speaks of your wisdom (even the eyebrows that you let me pluck ☺) Dad, your patience (not so much in driving but you have been working so hard at it. Way to go!) with Mom, Lauren, Amanda, and I speak of your character and your relationship with the Lord. You are constantly serving our family whether it be financially at work, physically doing things around the house, or emotionally and spiritually through conversations. Thank you for working so hard and for providing for our family. Your hard work and strong work ethic are things I hope to implement in my life and pass on to my children. Thank you for always being a man of integrity, strength, honor, and humility. You are in the words of Paul a very classy man's man who loves the Lord a lot! Thank you for encouraging me and my walk with the Christ. Your commitment to your guys at church (I helped lead a group of young men in High School ministry at the time) *is neat and very admirable. Thank you for pouring into them and building the Lord's kingdom by investing in these young men's lives. Thank you for being protective, cherishing me as your daughter and taking your role as a father seriously. Your*

love notes (now texts) are genuine, thoughtful, and a valued part in my day. I love you, Dad, and I am so thankful for you. May the Lord bless you on this special day! Happy Father's Day Daddy! I love you!

Love, Heather

Amanda was our pacifier addict. She always had her "Bink" as we called it where ever she went. As she grew older, we got to the point where Debbie and I limited her "Bink Time" to bedtime, naps and car rides. Amanda constantly pushed boundaries but had a knack for always staying just far enough inside the line as to not officially challenge authority. For example, she would play for awhile but when she needed some "Bink Time", she would go into her room, reach into her crib, grab Bink, and drag on it for a minute or two while *leaning against the crib*. She would then put it back in her bed and go off and play, repeating the same cycle multiple times throughout the day. Now I know, she wasn't going to bed, napping or in the car seat and in reality was in violation of our rule. OK, you caught me! I was not 100% consistent with my parenting. Guilty as charged. You see, I am not an expert and did not always do things *completely* correct! But come on, you have to give 3-year-old Amanda some credit for her creativity! Perhaps we could have used this as a defining moment, but her cute little grin as she would return the Bink to bed before returning to play was too much! Clever, very clever. Eventually Amanda approached the age where she would need to give up her precious Bink, and Debbie and I were contemplating how best to do this. One day I was outside watching her two older sisters play on a small 5 foot diameter trampoline that stood about a foot off the ground. Amanda shows up outside with you guessed it, Bink in mouth. I gave her the benefit of the doubt (a little mercy and grace) and calmly reminded her of our rule (Plan-Options-Emotion)..."No" was her response. What! Are you serious? This was no mere bending of the rule. This was complete disregard for parental authority. Amanda then proceeded to cut in front of sister Heather and climbed up on the trampoline. So much for "taking turns" either. Amanda was then the recipient of my calm explanation as to why it was dangerous to be jumping on the trampoline with her "Bink" not to mention she needed to return at once to her room to put Bink back to bed, or she would loose Bink..."No" with the sweet but telltale stare of defiance into my eyes. So this was the day. After a deep breath, I went over to Amanda, gently pulled the plug, and sent Bink over the wooden fence and into the alley never to be seen again. I then picked Amanda off the trampoline (since it was Heather's turn!), gave her a hug, and praised her for being a big girl now that her Bink was no longer needed. We then walked into the house, and I had her explain to her disbelieving Mom why she no longer had her Bink. I also had her apologize to her sister for cutting in front of her. Thankfully she complied or we would have had another "discipline" opportunity on our hands! A few summary points:

So what was the result? Well from then on, Amanda understood that Dad and Mom were in charge, that they were willing defend the boundaries we established, that they were willing to sacrifice whatever was needed (even precious Bink), and overtime she came to understand that the boundaries Debbie and I set were meant for her benefit. Did she ever challenge our authority again and did we have to reinforce this concept? Of course. Especially the first time she asked for Bink again, and we had to remind her it was gone! But this day *began* Amanda's understanding that she was the child, and Debbie and I were the parents. Yes this cost Amanda her Bink and Debbie and I several fussy, tearful reminders for awhile that Bink was gone for good, but we gained a beginning of a life-long understanding of parental authority. Did we pay the cost or enjoy a lifetime of benefit? I'll let you be the judge.

2010 Father's Day Card from Amanda...with her permission of course

Dear Daddy,
Thanks so much for being the great father that the Lord has planned you to be! You have given me wisdom and love; encouraged me through my whole life, and protected me, provided for me as a loving father! May the Lord bless you because you live a life that seeks only His will! You are my Hero! I love you so so so much and hope you have a joyful Father's Day!

With Love, Amanda

Important note: I share the Father's Day notes from our daughters for several reasons:

1. For you to get a glimpse of our home life from the children's perspective now that they are young adults

2. So you can see that anything good, anything praiseworthy that is coming from me (or Debbie) as a parent is from the Lord, and this only happens when we submit to His Lordship and allow Him to live in and through us.

3. **To God be the Glory!!** I am simply passing on to others what He has poured into my life.

Conclusion

"So what is a 'yoke' anyway?" I never really explained the analogy that Jesus used in Matthew 11:28-30 and the purpose of the picture on the front cover. A yoke is an instrument of work. A yoke is a devise farmers use to secure two oxen or horses together side by side so that the two can pull together and accomplish the tasks necessary to have a productive, successful farm. A yoke in this analogy represents the "not easiness" of life. At the same time, a yoke represents "relationship". When we team together with others, we give and receive support, encouragement, and help; and life in turn becomes much easier. Jesus uses this analogy in Matthew 11 inviting each one of us to take His yoke, to be in relationship with, to be under His guidance, His wisdom, and His power. And if we choose to take His yoke, He promises to be with us every step of the way, to pull with us, and that His yoke is easy and His burden is light. How can an instrument of work be easy and not burdensome? That's a great question! All I can tell you is that Jesus is in the business of doing the impossible, to transform the hearts and lives of those who place their faith in Him and surrender to His Lordship. Jesus is the way, the truth, and the life...not only the simpler and easier life, but the ETERNAL life!

"This is eternal life, that they may know You, the only true God, and Jesus Christ whom You have sent."

John 17:3

Well you've made it to the end of the book. My hope is that you have found something of value to assist you in this journey called "life". I also hope you continue growing in your relationship with the Lord as well as all the other important relationships in your life through prayer, studying God's Word, and seeking trustworthy resources to better equip you to live life to the full. My parting prayer for you is Colossians 3:12-17:

"So, as those who have been chosen of God, holy and beloved, put on a heart of compassion, kindness, humility, gentleness and patience; bearing with one another, and forgiving each other, whoever has a complaint against anyone; just as the Lord forgave you, so also should you. Beyond all these things put on love, which is the perfect bond of unity. Let the peace of Christ rule in your hearts, to which indeed you were called in one body; and be thankful. Let the word of Christ richly dwell within you, with all wisdom teaching and admonishing one another with psalms and hymns and spiritual songs, singing with thankfulness in your hearts to God. Whatever you do in word or deed, do all in the name of the Lord Jesus, giving thanks through Him to God the Father."

Amen

Additional Resources

Christianity

- ***The Bible*** by God (my preference: NASB or NIV)
- ***Basic Christianity*** by John R.W. Stott
- ***Case for Christ*** by Lee Strobel
- ***Grace Walk*** by Steve McVey
- ***So What's the Difference?*** by Fritz Ridenour
- ***The Purpose Driven Life*** by Rick Warren

Relationships / Personalities

- ***The Bible...*** by God (my preference: NASB or NIV)
- ***Personality Plus*** by Florence Littauer
- ***Insights (Personality Profile)*** founded by Andi and Andy Lothian and based on the work of Swiss psychologist Dr. Carl G Jung
- ***Boundaries Face to*** Face by Dr. Henry Cloud and Dr. John Townsend
- ***Five Love Languages*** by Gary Chapman

Marriage

- ***The Bible...*** by God (my preference: NASB or NIV)
- ***Hope for the Family...***Dr. Marlin Howe
- ***Growing Kids God's Way...***Gary and Anne Marie Ezzo

- ***Boundaries: Face to Face...***Dr. Henry Cloud and Dr. John Townsend
- ***Personality Plus...***Florence Littauer

Parenting

- ***The Bible...*** by God (my preference: NASB or NIV)
- ***Growing Kids God's Way....***by Gary and Anne Marie Ezzo
- ***The Power of Teachable Moments...***by Jim Weidmann & Marianne Hering

This is by no means an exhaustive list. These are resources that the Muir's have personally found beneficial to our family.

Study Sessions

Chapter 1: Purpose (pages 1-20)

I.   Expectations

What are your expectations in life as to the following roles?
From what source did your expectations originate?

People in General:

Friends:

Coworker/Teammate:

Spouse:

Parent:

II.   Audience

1. Who is your audience right now: friends, family, people
    at work, or are you a parent and have children watching
    you?

2. What kind of package would describe you: A or B or
    perhaps a bit of both? Why?

III. Discloser

1. Was there a time when other people helped you through a trial?

2. Has Jesus Christ ever carried you through a trial?

3. Is God resident or president of your life right now?

4. What are some things that I can do daily to make sure God is President of my life?

IV. Motivation

1. What one piece of advice would you want to pass on to the next generation?

2. What is required to be successful in sports, education, finances, and relationships? Do you have a personal testimony of a favorable or unfavorable outcome you are willing to share?

3. What problems do you enjoy solving and who or what do they involve?

4. What problems do you solve on a regular basis? Which ones would you rather someone else solve for you? Why?

5. Have you had an Acts 20:35 experience? What did you give? How were you blessed?

6. Would you use the word "glory" to describe your life? Why or why not?

7. What are you seeking from *"Life is Simple...It's Just Not Easy"*?

Study Session

Chapter 2: Perspective (pages 21-30)

1. From what perspective do you see: half full, half empty, or both?

2. What is consuming your "worldly cup" and is there anything you need to add or remove?

3. Am I comparing my patch of grass to my neighbor's? Do I think that theirs is greener?

4. Who is Jesus Christ in my life?

5. Have I received Jesus Christ and if so, do I live out my life accordingly? How full is my "spiritual glass"?

6. Do I live as if planet earth is my home or do I live as if Heaven is my home with an eternal point of view?

7. What if anything is holding you back from living with an eternal perspective? Fill in the blank.

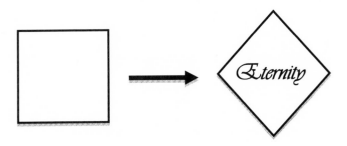

Study Session

Chapter 3: Priorities (pages 31-68)

Relationships

1. What relationships are most important to you? Why?

2. How have relationships formed your beliefs, values, and ultimately your actions?

3. Where do I get my relational security and significance from? When was I the most relationally secure and/or significant in my life? Why?

4. Have you been through a difficult situation that ultimately turned out for good?   If so, when did you recognize that it was meant for something "good"?

J-O-Y

1. Do I live out the "J-O-Y" principle? What will life look like if I live out the reverse of this acronym?

2. Is your goal to be happy or joyful? What's the difference?

3. What direction am I rolling down? What specific decisions did I make to roll in that direction?

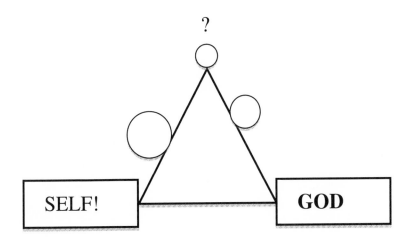

Forgiveness

1. Describe the following in your own words with an example from your own life...

   Offering Forgiveness:

   Receiving Forgiveness:

   Repentance:

   Restoration:

2. What are the three different approaches to forgiveness and repentance and which of the three do you practice more often?

   1_____
   2_____
   3_____

3. Who is someone you trust? Has that person ever given you a reason to doubt their trust? Did that person ever regain your trust? How? How long did that take?

4. Is there someone you need to forgive or repent to today? What is holding you back? Don't wait!!

Study Session

Chapter 4: Practically Speaking (pages 69 - 98)

Winning

1. Write in your own words the difference between loosing and getting beaten?

2. Write an example of a time when you lost and now reflecting on it, how would you change what you did?

The Package Deal

1. With the following list of topics, rank which ones are most important to you. Write in the blank what will influence your choice the most:

Attitude

Car

College/Education

Where you live

Your spouse

Home

Children / how many

Faith or belief system

2. When you make a choice, do you accept the whole "package"?

Complaining

1. Do you complain? How often? What do you complain about? Why? How does your complaining help or hurt your circumstance?

2. Have you ever been part of a problem or part of a solution? If so, which do you prefer? Why?

3. Do you avoid "unwholesome talk" and strive to build others up to the benefit of those around you (Eph 4:29)?

4. We reap what we sow. Give an example of something you want to harvest in your life? Are you willing to do

what is necessary to plant whatever it is that you want to harvest?

Freedom

1. What are you currently free from?

2. What would you like to be free from in the future?

3. Do you know how to free yourself in those areas of your life that confine you? Who can you turn to for help?

4. Think of a person you know who needs freedom and pray for them to find freedom in their life. Write a small prayer request and pray for them daily.

Study Sessions

Chapter 5 (pages 99 - 128)

Marriage

1. If marriage was the last and most important "final exam" that you needed to pass in order to graduate, how well prepared are you?

2. What is the primary need for most Gentlemen? Where do they typically find it? Where would you recommend they find it? (Eph 5:25-28) Why?

    NEED:

    WHERE:

3. What is the primary need for most Ladies? Where do they typically find it? Where would you recommend they find it? (Eph 5: 22-24) Why?

    NEED:

    WHERE:

4. Fill in the blank

   Goal-oriented activities provide _____
   Process- oriented activities provide _____
   in relationships.

5. Who will my marriage affect both now and in the future?

6. All marriages require effort, sacrifice, struggle, forgiveness, and growth. This can be uncomfortable. List an example in either your marriage or in another marriage where growth occurred from uncomfortable situations.

7. How would you define a "successful" marriage?

8. Do you have a short-term or long-term view on marriage? Why?

9. What binds a marriage together? How does the "marriage covenant" work?

10. If you are married or may be some day, what do you want at the center of your marriage? Why?

Parenting

1. Who has all the answers with regard to parenting? Who has all the answer for everything for that matter!

2. In your own words, children are the following and how?

   Gifts from God:

   Individual people:

   Family members:

3. How would you define "successful" parenting?

Study Sessions

Chapter 6: Practical Parenting Applications
(pages 129 - 168)

Survival is an Option

1. How do your choices lengthen the days of your life? If you are a parent, are you teaching this concept to your children? How?

2. Are there any choices in your life that might need adjusting to align with this concept?

Natural consequences

1. Fill in the consequence.
   Attend every practice and try your best:_____
   Skip practice: _____
   Attend class and study hard for the test:_____
   Don't study, cheat on a test: _____
   Follow the rules: _____
   Break the law: _____
   Pay your bills on time: _____
   Don't pay your taxes:_____
   Eat right, exercise, get adequate rest _____
   Eat unhealthy, don't exercise, get little rest _____

Stay in touch with friends: _____

Avoid friends unless you need something:_____

Discipline and train your children:_____

Avoid disciplining your children:_____

2. Obviously parents are to "protect" their children. Does "natural consequence" play a role in your parenting? What natural consequences are healthy for children to experience in order for them to mature into adulthood?

Discipline and training

1. If you don't discipline your children, who will do it for you?

2. Give an example of an incident that could be taught by the world instead of the parent. Which one do you think would be best for your children? Why?

Next Generation

1. Are you parenting for your generation, your children's generation, or the next?

2. The priority in parenting changes as your child matures. What is the priority in your parenting today? How will you know?

Relationship Priorities

1. How do you prioritize the relationships in your life and in particular, your family? What outcomes do you experience based upon these priorities?

2. Who leads your family? What influences the leader(s) in your family?

Plan-Options-Emotion

1. Do you seek ways to involve those important people in your life? How?

2. How well do you communicate with others, and in particular your children, in such a way as to allow them

to discern, make choices for themselves, and mature into adulthood?

Consistency

1 As the leader of the family, how are you at consistency? When you lead, is your family often "surprised" or do they have healthy, consistent boundaries along with consistent responses to certain behaviors?

2 For family leaders: imagine if you were a child in your family. How would you assess the leadership in your family? How would you respond to that leadership?

Alignment

1. Mom and Dad, do you discuss ahead of time what behaviors are important to your family along with the expectations and consequences of those behaviors?

2. Are you aligned, particularly on what is most important to your marriage?

Effective, Loving Discipline

1. What comes to mind when you hear the word "discipline"? What about "punishment"?

2. Do you embrace or avoid discipline situations in your life or in the lives of your children?

3. What is the difference between "discipline" and "punishment"? Why does the Lord "discipline those He loves"?

   Discipline:

   Punishment:

4. Have you clearly communicated healthy boundaries within your family? Do they know the consequences when those boundaries are followed or crossed?

The Pacifier Principal

1. What is the difference between a need and a want? How does this relate to "the Pacifier Principal"?

2. Thinking of your children's behavior, do you have any requirements in order for them to receive a "want"? What are your requirements?

Having a long-term perspective

1. Do you ever look upon your children as future adults, leaders, and parents of your grandchildren? Why or why not?

2. How might having a longer term perspective influence your parenting today?

Teenager is not an option

1 In your own words, how would you define a "teenager"?

2. Do you believe behaviors are encouraged? Why or why not?

3. What behaviors do you encourage in your life and in the lives of your family? How?

The Defining Moment

1. How would you describe the "defining moment"?

2. Have you ever experienced one? How did it influence your parenting?

3. How do you define success as a parent?

Study Sessions

Conclusion (pages 169 – 171)

1. Are you "yoked" and ready for life, marriage, and parenthood to the fullest?

2. Are you experiencing "eternal life"? Why or why not?

3. Reflect on Colossians 3:12-17. How might life be if we all lived "life to the full" (John 10:10b) in this manner?

4. What are some ways that you would like to grow in your relationships, marriage, and / or parenting? What is your next step?

Relationships:

Marriage:

Parenting:

Life is Simple…It's Just Not Easy

Nice Fish Publishing, LLC
www.nicefishpub.com
1-800-266-5564 (1-800-BOOKLOG)

NOTES:

NOTES: